THE RECONCILIATION OF RACES AND RELIGIONS

BY

THOMAS KELLY CHEYNE, D. LITT., D. D.

First published in 1914

Published by Left of Brain Books

Copyright © 2023 Left of Brain Books

ISBN 978-1-397-66536-2

First Edition

All rights reserved. No part of this publication may be reproduced, distributed, or transmitted in any form or by any means, including photocopying, recording, or other electronic or mechanical methods, without the prior written permission of the publisher, except in the case of brief quotations permitted by copyright law. Left of Brain Books is a division of Left Of Brain Onboarding Pty Ltd.

PUBLISHER'S PREFACE

About the Book

"The term race or racial group usually refers to the concept of dividing humans into populations or groups on the basis of various sets of characteristics. The most widely used human racial categories are based on visible traits (especially skin color, cranial or facial features and hair texture), and self-identification.

Conceptions of race, as well as specific ways of grouping races, vary by culture and over time, and are often controversial for scientific as well as social and political reasons. The controversy ultimately revolves around whether or not races are natural types or socially constructed, and the degree to which observed differences in ability and achievement, categorized on the basis of race, are a product of inherited (i.e. genetic) traits or environmental, social and cultural factors."

(Quote from wikipedia.org)

About the Author

"Sir Thomas Cheney, KG (c 1485 - December 15, 1558), or Cheyne, was Lord Warden of the Cinque Ports in South-East England, from 1536 until his death.

Thomas was born around 1485 at Shurland House, Eastchurch on the Isle of Sheppey in Kent, the son of William Cheney by his second wife, Agnes (or Margaret) Young. His uncle and guardian was John, Baron Cheney of Shurland, Henry VII's standard-bearer at the Battle of Bosworth Field. Thomas Cheney was knighted in 1513. Of his three brothers, Francis Cheney was a Governor of Queenborough Castle, Isle of Sheppey.

He was a favourite of Henry VIII's fiancee, Anne Boleyn, and she fought Cardinal Wolsey for his promotion in 1528 and 1529. However, it was not until 1535-40 that Cheney consolidated his authority as one of the most powerful men in the south-east of England."

(Quote from wikipedia.org)

CONTENTS

PUBLISHER'S PREFACE
PREFACE 1
INTRODUCTION 4
   THE JEWELS OF THE FAITHS 9
   BIOGRAPHICAL AND HISTORICAL 31
   BIOGRAPHICAL AND HISTORICAL (CONTINUED) 83
   BIOGRAPHICAL AND HISTORICAL; AMBASSADOR TO HUMANITY 94
   A SERIES OF ILLUSTRATIVE STUDIES BEARING ON COMPARATIVE RELIGION
   101
BAHAI BIBLIOGRAPHY 126

PREFACE

THE primary aim of this work is twofold. It would fain contribute to the cause of universal peace, and promote the better understanding of the various religions which really are but one religion. The union of religions must necessarily precede the union of races, which at present is so lamentably incomplete. It appears to me that none of the men or women of good-will is justified in withholding any suggestions which may have occurred to him. For the crisis, both political and religious, is alarming.

The question being ultimately a religious one, the author may be pardoned if he devotes most of his space to the most important of its religious aspects. He leaves it open to students of Christian politics to make known what is the actual state of things, and how this is to be remedied. He has, however, tried to help the reader by reprinting the very noble Manifesto of the Society of Friends, called forth by the declaration of war against Germany by England on the fourth day of August 1914.

In some respects I should have preferred a Manifesto representing the lofty views of the present Head of another Society of Friends--the Bahai Fraternity. Peace on earth has been the ideal of the Babis and Bahais since the Babs time, and Professor E. G. Browne has perpetuated Baha-'ullah's noble declaration of the imminent setting up of the kingdom of God, based upon universal peace. But there is such a thrilling actuality in the Manifesto of the Disciples of George Fox that I could not help availing myself of Mr. Isaac Sharp's kind permission to me to reprint it. It is indeed an opportune setting forth of the eternal riches, which will commend itself, now as never before, to those who can say, with the Grandfather in Tagore's poem, 'I am a jolly pilgrim to the land of losing everything.' The rulers of this world certainly do not cherish this ideal; but the imminent reconstruction of international relations will have to be founded upon it if we are not to sink back into the gulf of militarism.

I have endeavoured to study the various races and religions on their best side, and not to fetter myself to any individual teacher or party, for 'out of His fulness have all we received.' Max Müller was hardly right in advising the Brahmists to call themselves Christians, and it is a pity that we so habitually speak of Buddhists and Mohammedans. I venture to remark that the favourite name of the Bahais among themselves is 'Friends.' The ordinary name Bahai comes from the divine name Baha, 'Glory (of God),' so that Abdu'l Baha means 'Servant of the Glory (of God).' One remembers the beautiful words of the Latin collect, 'Cui servire regnare est.'

Abdu'l Baha (when in Oxford) graciously gave me a 'new name.' [1] Evidently he thought that my work was not entirely done, and would have me be ever looking for help to the Spirit, whose 'strength is made perfect in weakness.' Since then he has written me a Tablet (letter), from which I quote the following lines:--

'O thou, my spiritual philosopher,

'Thy letter was received. In reality its contents were eloquent, for it was an evidence of thy literary fairness and of thy investigation of Reality.... There were many Doctors amongst the Jews, but they were all earthly, but St. Paul became heavenly because he could fly upwards. In his own time no one duly recognized him; nay, rather, he spent his days amidst difficulties and contempt. Afterwards it became known that he was not an earthly bird, he was a celestial one; he was not a natural philosopher, but a divine philosopher.

'It is likewise my hope that in the future the East and the West may become conscious that thou wert a divine philosopher and a herald to the Kingdom.'

I have no wish to write my autobiography, but may mention here that I sympathize largely with Vambéry, a letter from whom to Abdu'l Baha will be found farther on; though I should express my own adhesion to the Bahai leader in more glowing terms. Wishing to get nearer to a 'human-catholic' religion I have sought the privilege of simultaneous membership of several brotherhoods of Friends of God. It is my wish to show that both these and other homes of spiritual life are, when studied from the inside, essentially one, and that religions necessarily issue in racial and world-wide unity.

RUHANI.

---

[1] Ruhani ('spiritual').

OXFORD, *August* 1914.

INTRODUCTION

TO MEN AND WOMEN OF GOODWILL IN THE BRITISH EMPIRE

A Message (reprinted by permission) from the Religious Society of Friends

WE find ourselves to-day in the midst of what may prove to be the fiercest conflict in the history of the human race. Whatever may be our view of the processes which have led to its inception, we have now to face the fact that war is proceeding upon a terrific scale and that our own country is involved in it.

We recognize that our Government has made most strenuous efforts to preserve peace, and has entered into the war under a grave sense of duty to a smaller State, towards which we had moral and treaty obligations. While, as a Society, we stand firmly to the belief that the method of force is no solution of any question, we hold that the present moment is not one for criticism, but for devoted service to our nation.

What is to be the attitude of Christian men and women and of all who believe in the brotherhood of humanity? In the distress and perplexity of this new situation, many are so stunned as scarcely to be able to discern the path of duty. In the sight of God we should seek to get back to first principles, and to determine on a course of action which shall prove us to be worthy citizens of His Kingdom. In making this effort let us remember those groups of men and women, in all the other nations concerned, who will be animated by a similar spirit, and who believe with us that the fundamental unity of men in the family of God is the one enduring reality, even when we are forced into an apparent denial of it. Although it would be premature to make any pronouncement upon many aspects of the situation on which we have no sufficient data for a reliable judgment, we can, and do, call ourselves and you to a consideration of certain principles which may safely be enunciated.

1. The conditions which have made this catastrophe possible must be regarded by us as essentially unchristian. This war spells the bankruptcy of much that we too lightly call Christian. No nation, no Church, no individual

can be wholly exonerated. We have all participated to some extent in these conditions. We have been content, or too little discontented, with them. If we apportion blame, let us not fail first to blame ourselves, and to seek the forgiveness of Almighty God.

2. In the hour of darkest night it is not for us to lose heart. Never was there greater need for men of faith. To many will come the temptation to deny God, and to turn away with despair from the Christianity which seems to be identified with bloodshed on so gigantic a scale. Christ is crucified afresh to-day. If some forsake Him and flee, let it be more clear that there are others who take their stand with Him, come what may.

3. This we may do by continuing to show the spirit of love to all. For those whose conscience forbids them to take up arms there are other ways of serving, and definite plans are already being made to enable them to take their full share in helping their country at this crisis. In pity and helpfulness towards the suffering and stricken in our own country we shall all share. If we stop at this, 'what do we more than others?' Our Master bids us pray for and love our enemies. May we be saved from forgetting that they too are the children of our Father. May we think of them with love and pity. May we banish thoughts of bitterness, harsh judgments, the revengeful spirit. To do this is in no sense unpatriotic. We may find ourselves the subjects of misunderstanding. But our duty is clear--to be courageous in the cause of love and in the hate of hate. May we prepare ourselves even now for the day when once more we shall stand shoulder to shoulder with those with whom we are now at war, in seeking to bring in the Kingdom of God.

4. It is not too soon to begin to think out the new situation which will arise at the close of the war. We are being compelled to face the fact that the human race has been guilty of a gigantic folly. We have built up a culture, a civilization, and even a religious life, surpassing in many respects that of any previous age, and we have been content to rest it all upon a foundation of sand. Such a state of society cannot endure so long as the last word in human affairs is brute force. Sooner or later it was bound to crumble. At the close of this war we shall be faced with a stupendous task of reconstruction. In some ways it will be rendered supremely difficult by the legacy of ill-will, by the destruction of human life, by the tax upon all in meeting the barest wants of the millions who will have suffered through the war. But in other ways it will be easier. We shall be able to make a new start,

and to make it all together. From this point of view we may even see a ground of comfort in the fact that our own nation is involved. No country will be in a position which will compel others to struggle again to achieve the inflated standard of military power existing before the war. We shall have an opportunity of reconstructing European culture upon the only possible permanent foundation--mutual trust and good-will. Such a reconstruction would not only secure the future of European civilization, but would save the world from the threatened catastrophe of seeing the great nations of the East building their new social order also upon the sand, and thus turning the thought and wealth needed for their education and development into that which could only be a fetter to themselves and a menace to the West. Is it too much to hope for that we shall, when the time comes, be able as brethren together to lay down far-reaching principles for the future of mankind such as will ensure us for ever against a repetition of this gigantic folly? If this is to be accomplished it will need the united and persistent pressure of all who believe in such a future for mankind. There will still be multitudes who can see no good in the culture of other nations, and who are unable to believe in any genuine brotherhood among those of different races. Already those who think otherwise must begin to think and plan for such a future if the supreme opportunity of the final peace is not to be lost, and if we are to be saved from being again sucked down into the whirlpool of military aggrandizement and rivalry. In time of peace all the nations have been preparing for war. In the time of war let all men of good-will prepare for peace. The Christian conscience must be awakened to the magnitude of the issues. The great friendly democracies in each country must be ready to make their influence felt. Now is the time to speak of this thing, to work for it, to pray for it.

5. If this is to happen, it seems to us of vital importance that the war should not be carried on in any vindictive spirit, and that it should be brought to a close at the earliest possible moment. We should have it clearly before our minds from the beginning that we are not going into it in order to crush and humiliate any nation. The conduct of negotiations has taught us the necessity of prompt action in international affairs. Should the opportunity offer, we, in this nation, should be ready to act with promptitude in demanding that the terms suggested are of a kind which it will be possible for all parties to accept, and that the negotiations be entered upon in the right spirit.

6. We believe in God. Human free will gives us power to hinder the fulfilment of His loving purposes. It also means that we may actively co-operate with Him. If it is given to us to see something of a glorious possible future, after all the desolation and sorrow that lie before us, let us be sure that sight has been given us by Him. No day should close without our putting up our prayer to Him that He will lead His family into a new and better day. At a time when so severe a blow is being struck at the great causes of moral, social, and religious reform for which so many have struggled, we need to look with expectation and confidence to Him, whose cause they are, and find a fresh inspiration in the certainty of His victory.

August 7, 1914.

'In time of war let all men of good-will prepare for peace.' German, French, and English scholars and investigators have done much to show that the search for truth is one of the most powerful links between the different races and nations. It is absurd to speak--as many Germans do habitually speak--of 'deutsche Wissenschaft,' as if the glorious tree of scientific and historical knowledge were a purely German production. Many wars like that which closed at Sedan and that which is still, most unhappily, in progress will soon drive lovers of science and culture to the peaceful regions of North America!

The active pursuit of truth is, therefore, one of those things which make for peace. But can we say this of moral and religious truth? In this domain are we not compelled to be partisans and particularists? And has not liberal criticism shown that the religious traditions of all races and nations are to be relegated to the least cultured classes? That is the question to the treatment of which I (as a Christian student) offer some contributions in the present volume. But I would first of all express my hearty sympathy with the friends of God in the noble Russian Church, which has appointed the following prayer among others for use at the present crisis: [1]

'*Deacon.* Stretch forth Thine hand, O Lord, from on high, and touch the hearts of our enemies, that they may turn unto Thee, the God of peace Who lovest Thy creatures: and for Thy Name's sake strengthen us who put our trust in Thee by Thy might, we beseech Thee. Hear us and have mercy.'

---

[1] *Church Times*, Sept. 4, 1914.

Certainly it is hardness of heart which strikes us most painfully in our (we hope) temporary enemies. The only excuse is that in the Book which Christian nations agree to consider as in some sense and degree religiously authoritative, the establishment of the rule of the Most High is represented as coincident with extreme severities, or--as we might well say--cruelties. I do not, however, think that the excuse, if offered, would be valid. The Gospels must overbear any inconsistent statement of the Old Testament.

But the greatest utterances of human morality are to be found in the Buddhist Scriptures, and it is a shame to the European peoples that the Buddhist Indian king Asoka should be more Christian than the leaders of 'German culture.' I for my part love the old Germany far better than the new, and its high ideals would I hand on, filling up its omissions and correcting its errors. 'O house of Israel, come ye, let us walk in the light of the Lord.' Thou art 'the God of peace Who lovest Thy creatures.'

THE JEWELS OF THE FAITHS

A STUDY OF THE CHIEF RELIGIONS ON THEIR BEST SIDE WITH A VIEW TO THEIR EXPANSION AND ENRICHMENT AND TO AN ULTIMATE SYNTHESIS AND TO THE FINAL UNION OF RACES AND NATIONS ON A SPIRITUAL BASIS

THE crisis in the Christian Church is now so acute that we may well seek for some mode of escape from its pressure. The Old Broad Church position is no longer adequate to English circumstances, and there is not yet in existence a thoroughly satisfactory new and original position for a Broad Church student to occupy. Shall we, then, desert the old historic Church in which we were christened and educated? It would certainly be a loss, and not only to ourselves. Or shall we wait with drooping head to be driven out of the Church? Such a cowardly solution may be at once dismissed. Happily we have in the Anglican Church virtually no excommunication. Our only course as students is to go forward, and endeavour to expand our too narrow Church boundaries. Modernists we are; modernists we will remain; let our only object be to be worthy of this noble name.

But we cannot be surprised that our Church rulers are perplexed. For consider the embarrassing state of critical investigation. Critical study of the Gospels has shown that very little of the traditional material can be regarded as historical; it is even very uncertain whether the Galilean prophet really paid the supreme penalty as a supposed enemy of Rome on the shameful cross. Even apart from the problem referred to, it is more than doubtful whether critics have left us enough stones standing in the life of Jesus to serve as the basis of a christology or doctrine of the divine Redeemer. And yet one feels that a theology without a theophany is both dry and difficult to defend. We want an avatâr, i.e. a 'descent' of God in human form; indeed, we seem to need several such 'descents,' appropriate to the changing circumstances of the ages. Did not the author of the Fourth Gospel recognize this? Certainly his portrait of Jesus is so widely different from that of the Synoptists that a genuine reconciliation seems impossible. I would not infer from this that the Jesus of the Fourth Gospel belonged to a different age from the Jesus of the Synoptists, but I would venture to say that the Fourth Evangelist would be easier to defend if he held this theory. The Johannine Jesus ought to have belonged to a different aeon.

ANOTHER IMAGE OF GOD

Well, then, it is reasonable to turn for guidance and help to the East. There was living quite lately a human being of such consummate excellence that many think it is both permissible and inevitable even to identify him mystically with the invisible Godhead. Let us admit, such persons say, that Jesus was the very image of God. But he lived for his own age and his own people; the Jesus of the critics has but little to say, and no redemptive virtue issues from him to us. But the 'Blessed Perfection,' as Baha'ullah used to be called, lives for our age, and offers his spiritual feast to men of all peoples. His story, too, is liable to no diminution at the hands of the critics, simply because the facts of his life are certain. He has now passed from sight, but he is still in the ideal world, a true image of God and a true lover of man, and helps forward the reform of all those manifold abuses which hinder the firm establishment of the kingdom of God. I shall return to this presently. Meanwhile, suffice it to say that though I entertain the highest reverence and love for Baha'ullah's son, Abdul Baha, whom I regard as a Mahatma--'a great-souled one'--and look up to as one of the highest examples in the spiritual firmament, I hold no brief for the Bahai community, and can be as impartial in dealing with facts relating to the Bahais as with facts which happen to concern my own beloved mother-church, the Church of England.

I shall first of all ask, how it came to pass that so many of us are now seeking help and guidance from the East, some from India, some from Persia, some (which is my own case) from India and from Persia.

BAHA'ULLAH'S PRECURSORS, *e.g.* THE BAB, SUFISM, AND SHEYKH AHMAD

So far as Persia is concerned, the reason is that its religious experience has been no less varied than ancient. Zoroaster, Manes, Christ, Muhammad, Dh'u-Nun (the introducer of Sufism), Sheykh Ahmad (the forerunner of Babism), the Bab himself and Baha'ullah (the two Manifestations), have all left an ineffaceable mark on the national life. The Bab, it is true, again and again expresses his repugnance to the 'lies' of the Sufis, and the Babis are not behind him; but there are traces enough of the influence of Sufism on the new Prophet and his followers. The passion for martyrdom seems of itself to presuppose a tincture of Sufism, for it is the most extreme form of the passion for God, and to love God fervently but steadily in preference to all the pleasures of the phenomenal world, is characteristically Sufite.

What is it, then, in Sufism that excites the Bab's indignation? It is not the doctrine of the soul's oneness with God as the One Absolute Being, and the reality of the soul's ecstatic communion with Him. Several passages are quoted by Mons. Nicolas [1] on the attitude of the Bab towards Sufism; suffice it here to quote one of them.

'Others (i.e. those who claim, as being identified with God, to possess absolute truth) are known by the name of Sufis, and believe themselves to possess the internal sense of the Shari'at [2] when they are in ignorance alike of its apparent and of its inward meaning, and have fallen far, very far from it! One may perhaps say of them that those people who have no understanding have chosen the route which is entirely of darkness and of doubt.'

Ignorance, then, is, according to the Bab, the great fault of the Sufis [3] whom he censures, and we may gather that that ignorance was thought to be especially shown in a crude pantheism and a doctrine of incarnation which, according to the Bab, amounts to sheer polytheism. [4] God in Himself, says the Bab, cannot be known, though a reflected image of Him is attainable by taking heed to His manifestations or perfect portraitures.

Some variety of Sufism, however, sweetly and strongly permeates the teaching of the Bab. It is a Sufism which consists, not in affiliation to any Sufi order, but in the knowledge and love of the Source of the Eternal Ideals. Through detachment from this perishable world and earnest seeking for the Eternal, a glimpse of the unseen Reality can be attained. The form of this only true knowledge is subject to change; fresh 'mirrors' or 'portraits' are provided at the end of each recurring cosmic cycle or aeon.

---

[1] *Beyan arabe*, pp. 3-18.
[2] The orthodox Law of Islam, which many Muslims seek to allegorize.
[3] Yet the title Sufi connotes knowledge. It means probably 'one who (like the Buddha on his statues) has a heavenly eye.' Prajnaparamita (*Divine Wisdom*) has the same third eye (Havell, *Indian Sculpture and Painting*, illustr. XLV.).
[4] The technical term is 'association.'

But the substance is unchanged and unchangeable. As Prof. Browne remarks, 'the prophet of a cycle is naught but a reflexion of the Primal Will,--the same sun with a new horizon.' [1]

THE BAB

Such a prophet was the Bab; we call him 'prophet' for want of a better name; 'yea, I say unto you, a prophet and more than a prophet.' His combination of mildness and power is so rare that we have to place him in a line with super-normal men. But he was also a great mystic and an eminent theosophic speculator. We learn that, at great points in his career, after he had been in an ecstasy, such radiance of might and majesty streamed from his countenance that none could bear to look upon the effulgence of his glory and beauty. Nor was it an uncommon occurrence for unbelievers involuntarily to bow down in lowly obeisance on beholding His Holiness; while the inmates of the castle, though for the most part Christians and Sunnis, reverently prostrated themselves whenever they saw the visage of His Holiness. [2] Such transfiguration is well known to the saints. It was regarded as the affixing of the heavenly seal to the reality and completeness of Bab's detachment. And from the Master we learn [3] that it passed to his disciples in proportion to the degree of their renunciation. But these experiences were surely characteristic, not only of Babism, but of Sufism. Ecstatic joy is the dominant note of Sufism, a joy which was of other-worldly origin, and compatible with the deepest tranquillity, and by which we are made like to the Ever-rejoicing One. The mystic poet Far'idu'd-din writes thus,--

> Joy! joy! I triumph now; no more I know
> Myself as simply me. I burn with love.
> The centre is within me, and its wonder
> Lies as a circle everywhere about me. [4]

And of another celebrated Sufi Sheykh (Ibnu'l Far'id) his son writes as follows: 'When moved to ecstasy by listening [to devotional recitations and

---

[1] *NH*, p. 335.
[2] *NH*, pp. 241, 242.
[3] Mirza Jani (*NH*, p. 242).
[4] Hughes, *Dict. of Islam*, p. 618 *b*.

chants] his face would increase in beauty and radiance, while the perspiration dripped from all his body until it ran under his feet into the ground.' [1]

EFFECT OF SUFISM

Sufism, however, which in the outset was a spiritual pantheism, combined with quietism, developed in a way that was by no means so satisfactory. The saintly mystic poet Abu Sa'id had defined it thus: 'To lay aside what thou hast in thy head (desires and ambitions), and to give away what thou hast in thy hand, and not to flinch from whatever befalls thee.' [2] This is, of course, not intended as a complete description, but shows that the spirit of the earlier Sufism was profoundly ethical. Count Gobineau, however, assures us that the Sufism which he knew was both enervating and immoral. Certainly the later Sufi poets were inclined to overpress symbolism, and the luscious sweetness of the poetry may have been unwholesome for some--both for poets and for readers. Still I question whether, for properly trained readers, this evil result should follow. The doctrine of the impermanence of all that is not God and that love between two human hearts is but a type of the love between God and His human creatures, and that the supreme happiness is that of identification with God, has never been more alluringly expressed than by the Sufi poets.

The Sufis, then, are true forerunners of the Bab and his successors. There are also two men, Muslims but no Sufis, who have a claim to the same title. But I must first of all do honour to an Indian Sufi.

INAYAT KHAN

The message of this noble company has been lately brought to the West.[3] The bearer, who is in the fulness of youthful strength, is Inayat Khan, a member of the Sufi Order, a practised speaker, and also devoted to the traditional sacred music of India. His own teacher on his death-bed gave him this affecting charge: 'Goest thou abroad into the world, harmonize the East and the West with thy music; spread the knowledge of Sufism, for thou art gifted by Allah, the Most Merciful and Compassionate.' So, then, Vivekananda, Abdu'l Baha, and Inayat Khan, not to mention here several

---

[1] Browne, *Literary History of Persia*, ii. 503.
[2] *Ibid*. ii. 208.
[3] *Message Soufi de la Liberté Spirituelle* (Paris, 1913).

Buddhist monks, are all missionaries of Eastern religious culture to Western, and two of these specially represent Persia. We cannot do otherwise than thank God for the concordant voice of Bahaite and Sufite. Both announce the Evangel of the essential oneness of humanity which will one day--and sooner than non-religious politicians expect--be translated into fact, and, as the first step towards this 'desire of all nations,' they embrace every opportunity of teaching the essential unity of religions:

> Pagodas, just as mosques, are homes of prayer,
> 'Tis prayer that church-bells chime unto the air;
> Yea, Church and Ka'ba, Rosary and Cross,
> Are all but divers tongues of world-wide prayer. [1]

So writes a poet (Omar Khayyám) whom Inayat Khan claims as a Sufi, and who at any rate seems to have had Sufi intervals. Unmixed spiritual prayer may indeed be uncommon, but we may hope that prayer with no spiritual elements at all is still more rare. It is the object of prophets to awaken the consciousness of the people to its spiritual needs. Of this class of men Inayat Khan speaks thus,--

'The prophetic mission was to bring into the world the Divine Wisdom, to apportion it to the world according to that world's comprehension, to adapt it to its degree of mental evolution as well as to dissimilar countries and periods. It is by this adaptability that the many religions which have emanated from the same moral principle differ the one from the other, and it is by this that they exist. In fact, each prophet had for his mission to prepare the world for the teaching of the prophet who was to succeed him, and each of them foretold the coming of his successor down to Mahomet, the last messenger of the divine Wisdom, and as it were the look-out point in which all the prophetic cycle was centred. For Mahomet resumed the divine Wisdom in this proclamation, "Nothing exists, God alone is,"--the final message whither the whole line of the prophets tended, and where the boundaries of religions and philosophies took their start. With this message prophetic interventions are henceforth useless.

'The Sufi has no prejudice against any prophet, and, contrary to those who only love one to hate the other, the Sufi regards them all as the highest attribute of God, as Wisdom herself, present under the appearance of

---

[1] Whinfield's translation of the quatrains of Omar Khayyám, No. 22 (34).

names and forms. He loves them with all his worship, for the lover worships the Beloved in all Her garments.... It is thus that the Sufis contemplate their Well-beloved, Divine Wisdom, in all her robes, in her different ages, and under all the names that she bears,--Abraham, Moses, Jesus, Mahomet.' [1]

The idea of the equality of the members of the world-wide prophethood, the whole body of prophets being the unique personality of Divine Wisdom, is, in my judgment, far superior to the corresponding theory of the exclusive Muhammadan orthodoxy. That theory is that each prophet represents an advance on his predecessor, whom he therefore supersedes. Now, that Muhammad as a prophet was well adapted to the Arabians, I should be most unwilling to deny. I am also heartily of opinion that a Christian may well strengthen his own faith by the example of the fervour of many of the Muslims. But to say that the Kur'an is superior to either the Old Testament or the New is, surely, an error, only excusable on the ground of ignorance. It is true, neither of Judaism nor of Christianity were the representatives in Muhammad's time such as we should have desired; ignorance on Muhammad's part was unavoidable. But unavoidable also was the anti-Islamic reaction, as represented especially by the Order of the Sufis. One may hope that both action and reaction may one day become unnecessary. *That* will depend largely on the Bahais.

It is time, however, to pass on to those precursors of Babism who were neither Sufites nor Zoroastrians, but who none the less continued the line of the national religious development. The majority of Persians were Shi'ites; they regarded Ali and the 'Imams' as virtually divine manifestations. This at least was their point of union; otherwise they fell into two great divisions, known as the 'Sect of the Seven' and the 'Sect of the Twelve' respectively. Mirza Ali Muhammad belonged by birth to the latter, which now forms the State-religion of Persia, but there are several points in his doctrine which he held in common with the former (i.e. the Ishma'ilis). These are--'the successive incarnations of the Universal Reason, the allegorical interpretation of Scripture, and the symbolism of every ritual form and every natural phenomenon. [2] The doctrine of the impermanence of all that is not God, and that love between two human hearts is but a type of the love between God and his human creatures, and the bliss of

---

[1] *Message Soufi de la Liberté* (Paris, 1913), pp. 34, 35.
[2] *NH*, introd. p. xiii.

self-annihilation, had long been inculcated in the most winning manner by the Sufis.

SHEYKH AHMAD

Yet they were no Sufis, but precursors of Babism in a more thorough and special sense, and both were Muslims. The first was Sheykh Ahmad of Ahsa, in the province of Bahrein. He knew full well that he was chosen of God to prepare men's hearts for the reception of the more complete truth shortly to be revealed, and that through him the way of access to the hidden twelfth Imam Mahdi was reopened. But he did not set this forth in clear and unmistakable terms, lest 'the unregenerate' should turn again and rend him. According to a Shi'ite authority he paid two visits to Persia, in one of which he was in high favour with the Court, and received as a yearly subsidy from the Shah's son the sum of 700 tumans, and in the other, owing chiefly to a malicious colleague, his theological doctrines brought him into much disrepute. Yet he lived as a pious Muslim, and died in the odour of sanctity, as a pilgrim to Mecca. [1]

One of his opponents (Mulla 'Ali) said of him that he was 'an ignorant man with a pure heart.' Well, ignorant we dare not call him, except with a big qualification, for his aim required great knowledge; it was nothing less than the reconciliation of all truth, both metaphysical and scientific. Now he had certainly taken much trouble about truth, and had written many books on philosophy and the sciences as understood in Islamic countries. We can only qualify our eulogy by admitting that he was unaware of the limitations of human nature, and of the weakness of Persian science. Pure in heart, however, he was; no qualification is needed here, except it be one which Mulla 'Ali would not have regarded as requiring any excuse. For purity he (like many others) understood In a large sense. It was the reward of courageous 'buffeting' and enslaving of the body; he was an austere ascetic.

He had a special devotion to Ja'far-i-Sadik,[2] the sixth Imam, whose guidance he believed himself to enjoy in dreams, and whose words he delighted to quote. Of course, 'Ali was the director of the council of the Imams, but the councillors were not much less, and were equally faithful as

---

[1] See *AMB* (Nicolas), pp. 264-272; *NH*, pp. 235, 236.
[2] *TN*, p. 297.

mirrors of the Supreme. This remains true, even if 'Ali be regarded as himself the Supreme God [1] identical with Allah or with the Ormazd (Ahura-Mazda) of the Zoroastrians. For the twelve Imams were all of the rank of divinities. Not that they were 'partners' with God; they were simply manifestations of the Invisible God. But they were utterly veracious Manifestations; in speaking of Allah (as the Sheykh taught) wer may venture to intend 'Ali. [2]

This explains how the Sheykh can have taught that the Imams took part in creation and are agents in the government of the world. In support of this he quoted Kur'an, Sur. xxiii. 14, 'God the best of Creators,' and, had he been a broader and more scientific theologian, might have mentioned how the Amshaspands (Ameshaspentas) are grouped with Ormazd in the creation-story of Zoroastrianism, and how, in that of Gen. i., the Director of the Heavenly Council says, 'Let *us* make man.' [3]

The Sheykh also believed strongly in the existence of a subtle body which survives the dissolution of the palpable, material body,[4] and will alone be visible at the Resurrection. Nothing almost gave more offence than this; it seemed to be only a few degrees better than the absolute denial of the resurrection-body ventured upon by the Akhbaris. [5] And yet the notion of a subtle, internal body, a notion which is Indian as well as Persian, has been felt even by many Westerns to be for them the only way to reconcile reason and faith.

SEYYID KAZIM--ISLAM--PARSIISM--BUDDHISM

On Ahmad's death the unanimous choice of the members of the school fell on Seyyid (Sayyid) Kazim of Resht, who had been already nominated by the Sheykh. He pursued the same course as his predecessor, and attracted many inquirers and disciples. Among the latter was the lady Kurratu'l 'Ayn,

---

[1] The Sheykh certainly tended in the direction of the sect of the 'Ali-Ilabis (*NH*, p. 142; Kremer, *Herrschende Ideen des Islams*, p. 31), who belonged to the *ghulat* or extreme Shi'ites (Browne, *Lit. Hist. of Persia*, p. 310).
[2] The Sheykh held that in reciting the opening *sura* of the Kur'an the worshipper should think of 'Ali, should intend 'Ali, as his God.
[3] Genesis i. 22.
[4] *TN*, p. 236.
[5] Gobineau, pp. 39, 40.

born in a town where the Sheykhi sect was strong, and of a family accustomed to religious controversy. He was not fifty when he died, but his career was a distinguished one. Himself a Gate, he discerned the successor by whom he was to be overshadowed, and he was the teacher of the famous lady referred to. To what extent 'Ali Muhammad (the subsequent Bab) was instructed by him is uncertain. It was long enough no doubt to make him a Sheykhite and to justify 'Ali Muhammad in his own eyes for raising Sheykh Ahmad and the Seyyid Kazim to the dignity of Bab. [1]

There seems to be conclusive evidence that Seyyid Kazim adverted often near the close of life to the divine Manifestation which he believed to be at hand. He was fond of saying, 'I see him as the rising sun.' He was also wont to declare that the 'Proof' would be a youth of the race of Hashim, i.e. a kinsman of Muhammad, untaught in the learning of men. Of a dream which he heard from an Arab (when in Turkish Arabia), he said, 'This dream signifies that my departure from the world is near at hand'; and when his friends wept at this, he remonstrated with them, saying, 'Why are ye troubled in mind? Desire ye not that I should depart, and that the truth [in person] should appear?' [2]

I leave it an open question whether Seyyid Kazim had actually fixed on the person who was to be his successor, and to reflect the Supreme Wisdom far more brilliantly than himself. But there is no reason to doubt that he regarded his own life and labours as transitional, and it is possible that by the rising sun of which he loved to speak he meant that strange youth of Shiraz who had been an irregular attendant at his lectures. Very different, it is true, is the Muhammadan legend. It states that 'Ali Muhammad was present at Karbala from the death of the Master, that he came to an understanding with members of the school, and that after starting certain miracle-stories, all of them proceeded to Mecca, to fulfil the predictions which connected the Prophet-Messiah with that Holy City, where, with bared sabre, he would summon the peoples to the true God.

This will, I hope, suffice to convince the reader that both the Sufi Order and the Sheykhite Sect were true forerunners of Babism and Bahaism. He will also readily admit that, for the Sufis especially, the connexion with a church of so weak a historic sense was most unfortunate. It would be the best for

---

[1] *AMB*, pp. 91, 95; cp. *NH*, p. 342.
[2] *NH*, p. 31.

all parties if Muslims both within and without the Sufi Order accepted a second home in a church (that of Abha) whose historical credentials are unexceptionable, retaining membership of the old home, so as to be able to reform from within, but superadding membership of the new. Whether this is possible on a large scale, the future must determine. It will not be possible if those who combine the old home with a new one become themselves thereby liable to persecution. It will not even be desirable unless the new-comers bring with them doctrinal (I do not say dogmatic) contributions to the common stock of Bahai truths--contributions of those things for which alone in their hearts the immigrant Muslim brothers infinitely care.

It will be asked, What are, to a Muslim, and especially to a Shi'ite Muslim, infinitely precious things? I will try to answer this question. First of all, in time of trouble, the Muslim certainly values as a 'pearl of great price' the Mercifulness and Compassion of God. Those who believingly read the Kur'an or recite the opening prayer, and above all, those who pass through deep waters, cannot do otherwise. No doubt the strict justice of God, corresponding to and limited by His compassion, is also a true jewel. We may admit that the judicial severity of Allah has received rather too much stress; still there must be occasions on which, from earthly caricatures of justice pious Muslims flee for refuge in their thoughts to the One Just Judge. Indeed, the great final Judgment is, to a good Muslim, a much stronger incentive to holiness than the sensuous descriptions of Paradise, which indeed he will probably interpret symbolically.

The true Muslim will be charitable even to the lower animals.[1] Neither poor-law nor Society for the Protection of Animals is required in Muslim countries. How soon organizations arose for the care of the sick, and, in war-time, of the wounded, it would be difficult to say; for Buddhists and Hindus were of course earlier in the field than Muslims, inheriting as they did an older moral culture. In the Muslim world, however, the twelfth century saw the rise of the Kadirite Order, with its philanthropic procedure.[2] Into the ideal of man, as conceived by our Muslim brothers, there must therefore enter the feature of mercifulness. We cannot help sympathizing with this, even though we think Abdul Baha's ideal richer and nobler than any as yet conceived by any Muslim saint.

---

[1] Nicholson, *The Mystics of Islam*, p. 108.
[2] D. S. Margoliouth, *Mohammedanism*, pp. 211-212.

There is also the idea--the realized idea--of brotherhood, a brotherhood which is simply an extension of the equality of Arabian tribesmen. There is no caste in Islam; each believer stands in the same relation to the Divine Sovereign. There may be poor, but it is the rich man's merit to relieve them. There may be slaves, but slaves and masters are religiously one, and though there are exceptions to the general kindliness of masters and mistresses, it is in East Africa that these lamentable inconsistencies are mostly found. The Muslim brothers who may join the Bahais will not find it hard to shake off their moral weaknesses, and own themselves brothers of their servants. Are we not all (they will say) sons of Adam? Lastly, there is the character of Muhammad. Perfect he was not, but Baha'ullah was hardly quite fair to Muhammad when (if we may trust a tradition) he referred to the Arabian prophet as a camel-driver. It is a most inadequate description. He had a 'rare beauty and sweetness of nature' to which he joined a 'social and political genius' and 'towering manhood.' [1]

These are the chief contributions which Muslim friends and lovers will be able to make; these, the beliefs which we shall hold more firmly through our brothers' faith. Will Muslims accept as well as proffer gifts? Speaking of a Southern Morocco Christian mission, S. L. Bensusan admits that it does not make Christians out of Moors, but claims that it 'teaches the Moors to live finer lives within the limits of their own faith.' [2]

I should like to say something here about the sweetness of Muhammad. It appears not only in his love for his first wife and benefactress, Khadijah, but in his affection for his daughter, Fatima. This affection has passed over to the Muslims, who call her very beautifully 'the Salutation of all Muslims.' The Babis affirm that Fatima returned to life in their own great heroine.

There is yet another form of religion that I must not neglect--the Zoroastrian or Parsi faith. Far as this faith may have travelled from its original spirituality, it still preserved in the Bab's time some elements of truth which were bound to become a beneficial leaven. This high and holy faith (as represented in the Gathas) was still the religion of the splendour or glory of God, still the champion of the Good Principle against the Evil. As if to show his respectful sympathy for an ancient and persecuted religion the Bab borrowed some minor points of detail from his Parsi neighbours. Not

---

[1] Sister Nivedita, *The Web of Indian Life*, pp. 242, 243.
[2] *Morocco* (A. & C. Black), p. 164.

on these, however, would I venture to lay any great stress, but rather on the doctrines and beliefs in which a Parsi connexion may plausibly be held. For instance, how can we help tracing a parallel between 'Ali and the Imams on the one hand and Ahura-Mazda (Ormazd) and his council of Amshaspands (Amesha-spentas) on the other? The founders of both religions conceived it to be implied in the doctrine of the Divine Omnipresence that God should be represented in every place by His celestial councillors, who would counteract the machinations of the Evil Ones. For Evil Ones there are; so at least Islam holds. Their efforts are foredoomed to failure, because their kingdom has no unity or cohesion. But strange mystic potencies they have, as all pious Muslims think, and we must remember that 'Ali Muhammad (the Bab) was bred up in the faith of Islam.

Well, then, we can now proceed further and say that our Parsi friends can offer us gifts worth the having. When they rise in the morning they know that they have a great warfare to wage, and that they are not alone, but have heavenly helpers. This form of representation is not indeed the only one, but who shall say that we can dispense with it? Even if evil be but the shadow of good, a *Maya*, an appearance, yet must we not act as if it had a real existence, and combat it with all our might?

May we also venture to include Buddhism among the religions which may directly or indirectly have prepared the way for Bahaism? We may; the evidence is as follows. Manes, or Mani, the founder of the widely-spread sect of the Manichaeans, who lived in the third century of our era, writes thus in the opening of one of his books,-- [1]

'Wisdom and deeds have always from time to time been brought to mankind by the messengers of God. So in one age they have been brought by the messenger of God called Buddha to India, in another by Zoroaster to Persia, in another by Jesus to the West. Thereafter this revelation has come down, this prophecy in this last age, through me, Mani, the Messenger of the God of Truth to Babylonia' ('Irak).

This is valid evidence for at least the period before that of Mani. We have also adequate proofs of the continued existence of Buddhism in Persia in the eleventh, twelfth, and thirteenth centuries; indeed, we may even assert

---

[1] *Literary History of Persia*, i. 103.

this for Bactria and E. Persia with reference to nearly 1000 years before the Muhammadan conquest. [1]

Buddhism, then, battled for leave to do the world good in its own way, though the intolerance of Islam too soon effaced its footprints. There is still some chance, however, that Sufism may be a record of its activity; in fact, this great religious upgrowth may be of Indian rather than of Neoplatonic origin, so that the only question is whether Sufism developed out of the Vedanta or out of the religious philosophy of Buddhism. That, however, is too complex a question to be discussed here.

All honour to Buddhism for its noble effort. In some undiscoverable way Buddhists acted as pioneers for the destined Deliverer. Let us, then, consider what precious spiritual jewels its sons and daughters can bring to the new Fraternity. There are many most inadequate statements about Buddhism. Personally, I wish that such expressions as 'the cold metaphysic of Buddhism' might be abandoned; surely metaphysicians, too, have religious needs and may have warm hearts. At the same time I will not deny that I prefer the northern variety of Buddhism, because I seem to myself to detect in the southern Buddhism a touch of a highly-refined egoism. Self-culture may or may not be combined with self-sacrifice. In the case of the Buddha it was no doubt so combined, as the following passage, indited by him, shows--

'All the means that can be used as bases for doing right are not worth one sixteenth part of the emancipation of the heart through love. That takes all those up into itself, outshining them in radiance and in glory.' [2]

What, then, are the jewels of the Buddhist which he would fain see in the world's spiritual treasury?

He will tell you that he has many jewels, but that three of them stand out conspicuously--the Buddha, the Dharma, and the Sangha. Of these the first is 'Sakya Muni, called the Buddha (the Awakened One).' His life is full of legend and mythology, but how it takes hold of the reader! Must we not pronounce it the finest of religious narratives, and thank the scholars who made the *Lalita Vistara* known to us? The Buddha was indeed a supernor-

---

[1] R. A. Nicholson, *The Mystics*, p. 18. Cp. E. G. Browne, *Lit. Hist. of Persia*, ii. 440 *ff*.
[2] Mrs. Rhys Davids, *Buddhism*, p. 229.

mal man; morally and physically he must have had singular gifts. To an extraordinary intellect he joined the enthusiasm of love, and a thirst for service.

The second of the Buddhist brother's jewels is the Dharma, i.e. the Law or Essential Rightness revealed by the Buddha. That the Master laid a firm practical foundation for his religion cannot be denied, and if Jews and Christians reverence the Ten Words given through 'Moses,' much more may Buddhists reverence the ten moral precepts of Sakya Muni. Those, however, whose aim is Buddhaship (i.e. those who propose to themselves the more richly developed ideal of northern Buddhists) claim the right to modify those precepts just as Jesus modified the Law of Moses. While, therefore, we recognize that good has sometimes come even out of evil, we should also acknowledge the superiority of Buddhist countries and of India in the treatment both of other human beings and of the lower animals.

The Sangha, or Monastic Community, is the third treasure of Buddhism, and the satisfaction of the Buddhist laity with the monastic body is said to be very great. At any rate, the cause of education in Burma owes much to the monks, but it is hard to realize how the Monastic Community can be in the same sense a 'refuge' from the miseries of the world as the Buddha or Dharmakâya.

The name Dharmakâya [1] (Body of Dharma, or system of rightness) may strike strangely upon our ears, but northern Buddhism makes much of it, and even though it may not go back to Sakya Muni himself, it is a development of germs latent in his teaching; and to my own mind there is no more wonderful conception in the great religions than that of Dharmakâya. If any one attacks our Buddhist friends for atheism, they have only to refer (if they can admit a synthesis of northern and southern doctrines) to the conception of Dharmakâya, of Him who is 'for ever Divine and Eternal,' who is 'the One, devoid of all determinations.' 'This Body of Dharma,' we are told, 'has no boundary, no quarters, but is embodied in all bodies.... All forms of corporeality are involved therein; it is able to create all things. Assuming any concrete material form, as required by the nature and condition of karma, it illuminates all creations.... There is no place in the universe where this Body does not prevail. The universe becomes dust; this

---

[1] Johnston, *Buddhist China*, p. 77.

Body for ever remains. It is free from all opposites and contraries, yet it is working in all things to lead them to Nirvana.'[1]

In fact, this Dharmakâya is the ultimate principle of cosmic energy. We may call it principle, but it is not, like Brahman, absolutely impersonal. Often it assumes personality, when it receives the name of Tathagata. It has neither passions nor prejudices, but works for the salvation of all sentient beings universally. Love (*karunâ*) and intelligence (*bodhi*) are equally its characteristics. It is only the veil of illusion (*maya*) which prevents us from seeing Dharmakâya in its magnificence. When this veil is lifted, individual existences as such will lose their significance; they will become sublimated and ennobled in the oneness of Dharmakâya.[2]

Will the reader forgive me if I mention some other jewels of the Buddhist faith? One is the Buddha Ami'tabha, and the other Kuanyin or Kwannon, his son or daughter; others will be noted presently. The latter is especially popular in China and Japan, and is generally spoken of by Europeans as the 'Goddess of Mercy.' 'Goddess,' however, is incorrect, [3]just as 'God' would be incorrect in the case of Ami'tabha. Sakya Muni was considered greater than any of the gods. All such Beings were saviours and helpers to man, just as Jesus is looked up to by Christian believers as a saviour and deliverer, and perhaps I might add, just as there are, according to the seer-poet Dante, three compassionate women (*donne*) in heaven.[4] Kwannon and her Father may surely be retained by Chinese and Japanese, not as gods, but as gracious *bodhisatts* (i.e. Beings whose essence is intelligence).

I would also mention here as 'jewels' of the Buddhists (1) their tenderness for all living creatures. Legend tells of Sakya Muni that in a previous state of existence he saved the life of a doe and her young one by offering his own life as a substitute. In one of the priceless panels of Bôrôbudûr in Java this legend is beautifully used.[5] It must indeed have been almost more impressive to the Buddhists even than Buddha's precept.

---

[1] Suzuki, *Outlines*, pp. 223-24.
[2] *Ibid*. p. 179.
[3] Johnston, *Buddhist China*, p. 123.
[4] Dante, *D.C., Inf.* ii. 124 *f*. The 'blessed women' seem to be Mary (the mother of Christ), Beatrice, and Lucia.
[5] Havell, *Indian Sculpture and Painting*, p. 123.

E'en as a mother watcheth o'er her child,
Her only child, as long as life doth last,
So let us, for all creatures great or small,
Develop such a boundless heart and mind,
Ay, let us practise love for all the world,
Upward and downward, yonder, thence,
Uncramped, free from ill-will and enmity.[1]

(2 and 3) Faith in the universality of inspiration and a hearty admission that spiritual pre-eminence is open to women. As to the former, Suzuki has well pointed out that Christ is conceived of by Buddhists quite as the Buddha himself. [2]'The Dharmakâya revealed itself as Sakya Muni to the Indian mind, because that was in harmony with its needs. The Dharmakâya appeared in the person of Christ on the Semitic stage, because it suited their taste best in this way.' As to the latter, there were women in the ranks of the Arahats in early times; and, as the *Psalms of the Brethren* show, there were even child-Arahats, and, so one may presume, girl-Arahats. And if it is objected that this refers to the earlier and more flourishing period of the Buddhist religion, yet it is in a perfectly modern summary of doctrine that we find these suggestive words, [3]'With this desire even a maiden of seven summers [4] may be a leader of the four multitudes of beings.' That spirituality has nothing to do with the sexes is the most wonderful law in the teachings of the Buddhas.'

India being the home of philosophy, it is not surprising either that Indian religion should take a predominantly philosophical form, or that there should be a great variety of forms of Indian religion. This is not to say that the feelings were neglected by the framers of Indian theory, or that there is any essential difference between the forms of Indian religion. On the contrary, love and intelligence are inseparably connected in that religion and there are fundamental ideas which impart a unity to all the forms of Hindu religion. That form of religion, however, in which love (*karunâ*) receives the highest place, and becomes the centre conjointly with intelligence of a theory of emancipation and of perfect Buddhahood, is

---

[1] Mrs. Rhys Davids, *Buddhism*, p. 219.
[2] Suzuki, *Outlines of the Mahâyâna Buddhism*.
[3] Omoro in *Oxford Congress of Religions, Transactions*, i. 152.
[4] 'The age of seven is assigned to all at their ordination' (*Psalms of the Brethren*, p. xxx.) The reference is to child-Arahats.

neither Vedantism nor primitive Buddhism, but that later development known as the Mahâyâna. Germs indeed there are of the later theory; and how should there not be, considering the wisdom and goodness of those who framed those systems? How beautiful is that ancient description of him who would win the joy of living in Brahma (Tagore, *Sadhanâ*, p. 106), and not much behind it is the following passage of the Bhagavad-Gita, 'He who hates no single being, who is friendly and compassionate to all ... whose thought and reason are directed to Me, he who is [thus] devoted to Me is dear to Me' (Discourse xii. 13, 14). This is a fine utterance, and there are others as fine.

One may therefore expect that most Indian Vedantists will, on entering the Bahai Society, make known as widely as they can the beauties of the Bhagavad-Gita. I cannot myself profess that I admire the contents as much as some Western readers, but much is doubtless lost to me through my ignorance of Sanskrit. Prof. Garbe and Prof. Hopkins, however, confirm me in my view that there is often a falling off in the immediateness of the inspiration, and that many passages have been interpolated. It is important to mention this here because it is highly probable that in future the Scriptures of the various churches and sects will be honoured by being read, not less devotionally but more critically. Not the Bibles as they stand at present are revealed, but the immanent Divine Wisdom. Many things in the outward form of the Scriptures are, for us, obsolete. It devolves upon us, in the spirit of filial respect, to criticize them, and so help to clear the ground for a new prophet.

A few more quotations from the fine Indian Scriptures shall be given. Their number could be easily increased, and one cannot blame those Western admirers of the Gita who display almost as fervent an enthusiasm for the unknown author of the Gita as Dante had for his *savio duca* in his fearsome pilgrimage.

THE BHAGAVAD-GITA AND THE UPANISHADS

Such criticism was hardly possible in England, even ten or twenty years ago, except for the Old Testament. Some scholars, indeed, had had their eyes opened, but even highly cultured persons in the lay-world read the Bhagavad-Gita with enthusiastic admiration but quite uncritically. Much as I sympathize with Margaret Noble (Sister Nivedita), Jane Hay (of St. Abb's, Berwickshire, N.B.), and Rose R. Anthon, I cannot desire that their excessive love for the Gita should find followers. I have it on the best authority that the apparent superiority of the Indian Scriptures to those of the Christian world influenced Margaret Noble to become 'Sister Nivedita'--a great result from a comparatively small cause. And Miss Anthon shows an excess of enthusiasm when she puts these words (without note or comment) into the mouth of an Indian student:--

'But now, O sire, I have found all the wealth and treasure and honour of the universe in these words that were uttered by the King of Kings, the Lover of Love, the Giver of Heritages. There is nothing I ask for; no need is there in my being, no want in my life that this Gita does not fill to overflowing.' [1]

There are in fact numerous passages in the Gita which, united, would form a *Holy Living* and a *Holy Dying*, if we were at the pains to add to the number of the passages a few taken from the Upanishads. Vivekananda and Rabindranath Tagore have already studded their lectures with jewels from the Indian Scriptures. The Hindus themselves delight in their holy writings, but if these writings are to become known in the West, the grain must first be sifted. In other words, there must be literary and perhaps also (I say it humbly) moral criticism.

I will venture to add a few quotations:--

'Whenever there is a decay of religion, O Bhâratas, and an ascendency of irreligion, then I manifest myself.

'For the protection of the good, for the destruction of evildoers, for the firm establishment of religion, I am born in every age.'

The other passages are not less noble.

'They also who worship other gods and make offering to them with faith, O son of Kunti, do verily make offering to me, though not according to ordinance.'

'Never have I not been, never hast thou, and never shall time yet come when we shall not all be. That which pervades this universe is imperishable; there is none can make to perish that changeless being. This never is born,

---

[1] *Stories of India*, 1914, p. 138.

and never dies, nor may it after being come again to be not; this unborn, everlasting, abiding, Ancient, is not slain when the body is slain. Knowing This to be imperishable, everlasting, unborn, changeless, how and whom can a man make to be slain or slay? As a man lays aside outworn garments, and takes others that are new, so the Body-Dweller puts away outworn bodies and goes to others that are new. Everlasting is This, dwelling in all things, firm, motionless, ancient of days.'

JUDAISM

Judaism, too, is so rich in spiritual treasures that I hesitate to single out more than a very few jewels. It is plain, however, that it needs to be reformed, and that this need is present in many of the traditional forms which enshrine so noble a spiritual experience. The Sabbath, for instance, is as the apple of his eye to every true-hearted Jew; he addresses it in his spiritual songs as a Princess. And he does well; the title Princess belongs of right to 'Shabbath.' For the name--be it said in passing--is probably a corruption of a title of the Mother-goddess Ashtart, and it would, I think, have been no blameworthy act if the religious transformers of Israelite myths had made a special myth, representing Shabbath as a man. When the Messiah comes, I trust that *He* will do this. For 'the Son of Man is Lord also of the Sabbath.'

The faith of the Messiah is another of Israel's treasures. Or rather, perhaps I should say, the faith in the Messiahs, for one Messiah will not meet the wants of Israel or the world. The Messiah, or the Being-like-a-man (Dan. vii. 13), is a supernatural Being, who appears on earth when he is wanted, like the Logos. We want Messiah badly now; specially, I should say, we Christians want 'great-souled ones' (Mahatmas), who can 'guide us into all the truth' (John xvi. 13). That they have come in the past, I doubt not. God could not have left his human children in the lurch for all these centuries. One thousand Jews of Tihran are said to have accepted Baha'ullah as the expected Messiah. They were right in what they affirmed, and only wrong in what they denied. And are we not all wrong in virtually denying the Messiahship of women-leaders like Kurratu'l 'Ayn; at least, I have only met with this noble idea in a work of Fiona Macleod.

CHRISTIANITY

And what of our own religion?

What precious jewels are there which we can share with our Oriental brethren? First of all one may mention that wonderful picture of the divine-human Saviour, which, full of mystery as it is, is capable of attracting to its Hero a fervent and loving loyalty, and melting the hardest heart. We have also a portrait (implicit in the Synoptic Gospels)--the product of nineteenth century criticism--of the same Jesus Christ, and yet who could venture to affirm that He really was the same, or that a subtle aroma had not passed away from the Life of lives? In this re-painted portrait we have, no longer a divine man, but simply a great and good Teacher and a noble Reformer. This portrait too is in its way impressive, and capable of lifting men above their baser selves, but it would obviously be impossible to take this great Teacher and Reformer for the Saviour and Redeemer of mankind.

We have further a pearl of great price in the mysticism of Paul, which presupposes, not the Jesus of modern critics, nor yet the Jesus of the Synoptics, but a splendid heart-uplifting Jesus in the colours of mythology. In this Jesus Paul lived, and had a constant ecstatic joy in the everlasting divine work of creation. He was 'crucified with Christ,' and it was no longer Paul that lived, but Christ that lived in him. And the universe--which was Paul's, inasmuch as it was Christ's--was transformed by the same mysticism. 'It was,' says Evelyn Underhill,[1] 'a universe soaked through and through by the Presence of God: that transcendent-immanent Reality, "above all, and through all, and in you all" as fontal "Father," energising "Son," indwelling "Spirit," in whom every mystic, Christian or non-Christian, is sharply aware that "we live and move and have our being." To his extended consciousness, as first to that of Jesus, this Reality was more actual than anything else--"God is all in all."'

It is true, this view of the Universe as God-filled is probably not Paul's, for the Epistles to the Ephesians and Colossians are hardly that great teacher's work. But it is none the less authentic, 'God is all and in all'; the whole Universe is temporarily a symbol by which God is at once manifested and veiled. I fear we have largely lost this. It were therefore better to reconquer this truth by India's help. Probably indeed the initial realization of the divinity of the universe (including man) is due to an increased acquaintance with the East and especially with Persia and India.

---

[1] *The Mystic Way*, p. 194 (chap. iii. 'St. Paul and the Mystic Way').

And I venture to think that Catholic Christians have conferred a boon on their Protestant brethren by emphasizing the truth of the feminine element (see pp. 25, 28) in the manifestation of the Deity, just as the Chinese and Japanese Buddhists have done for China and Japan, and the modern reformers of Indian religion have done for India. This too is a 'gem of purest ray.'

BIOGRAPHICAL AND HISTORICAL

SEYYID 'ALI MUHAMMAD (THE BAB)

SEYYID 'Ali Muhammad was born at Hafiz' city. It was not his lot, however, to rival that great lyric poet; God had far other designs for him. Like St. Francis, he had a merchant for his father, but this too was widely apart from 'AH Muhammad's destiny, which was neither more nor less than to be a manifestation of the Most High. His birthday was on the 1st Muharrem, A.H. 1236 (March 26, A.D. 1821). His maternal uncle, [1] however, had to step in to take a father's place; he was early left an orphan. When eighteen or nineteen years of age he was sent, for commer-cial reasons, to Bushire, a place with a villainous climate on the Persian Gulf, and there he wrote his first book, still in the spirit of Shi'ite orthodoxy.

It was in A.D. 1844 that a great change took place, not so much in doctrine as in the outward framework of Ali Muhammad's life. That the twelfth Imam should reappear to set up God's beneficent kingdom, that his 'Gate' should be born just when tradition would have him to be born, was perhaps not really surprising; but that an ordinary lad of Shiraz should be chosen for this high honour was exciting, and would make May 23rd a day memorable for ever. [2]

It was, in fact, on this day (at 2.5 A.M.) that, having turned to God for help, he cried out, 'God created me to instruct these ignorant ones, and to save them from the error into which they are plunged.' And from this time we cannot doubt that the purifying west wind breathed over the old Persian land which needed it so sadly.

It is probable, however, that the reformer had different ideas of disciple-ship. In one of his early letters he bids his correspondent take care to conceal his religion until he can reveal it without fear. Among his chief

---

[1] This relative of the Bab is mentioned in Baha-'ullah's *Book of Ighan*, among the men of culture who visited Baha-'ullah at Baghdad and laid their difficulties before him. His name was Seyyid 'Ali Muhammad (the same name as the Bab's).

[2] *TN*, pp. 3 (n.1), 220 *f.*; cp. *AMB*, p. 204.

disciples were that gallant knight called the 'Gate's Gate,' Kuddus, and his kind uncle. Like most religious leaders he attached great worth to pilgrimages. He began by journeying to the Shi'ite holy places, consecrated by the events of the Persian Passion-play. Then he embarked at Bushire, accompanied (probably) by Kuddus. The winds, however, were contrary, and he was glad to rest a few days at Mascat. It is probable that at Mecca (the goal of his journey) he became completely detached from the Muhammadan form of Islam. There too he made arrangements for propaganda. Unfavourable as the times seemed, his disciples were expected to have the courage of their convictions, and even his uncle, who was no longer young, became a fisher of men. This, it appears to me, is the true explanation of an otherwise obscure direction to the uncle to return to Persia by the overland route, *via* Baghdad, 'with the verses which have come down from God.'

The overland route would take the uncle by the holy places of 'Irak; 'Ali [Muh.]ammad's meaning therefore really is that his kinsman is to have the honour of evangelizing the important city of Baghdad, and of course the pilgrims who may chance to be at Karbala and Nejef. These were, to Shi'ites, the holiest of cities, and yet the reformer had the consciousness that there was no need of searching for a *kibla*. God was everywhere, but if one place was holier than another, it was neither Jerusalem nor Mecca, but Shiraz. To this beautiful city he returned, nothing loth, for indeed the manners of the pilgrims were the reverse of seemly. His own work was purely spiritual: it was to organize an attack on a foe who should have been, but was no longer, spiritual.

Among his first steps was sending the 'First to Believe' to Isfahan to make a conquest of the learned Mulla Mukaddas. His expectation was fully realized. Mukaddas was converted, and hastened to Shiraz, eager to prove his zeal. His orders were (according to one tradition) to introduce the name of 'Ali Muhammad into the call to prayer (*azan*) and to explain a passage in the commentary on the Sura of Joseph. This was done, and the penalty could not be delayed. After suffering insults, which to us are barely credible, Mukaddas and his friend found shelter for three days in Shiraz in the Bab's house.

It should be noted that I here employ the symbolic name 'the Bab.' There is a traditional saying of the prophet Muhammad, 'I am the city of knowledge, and 'Ali is its Gate.' It seems, however, that there is little, if any, difference between 'Gate' (*Bab*) and 'Point' (*nukta*), or between either of these and 'he who shall arise' (*ka'im*) and 'the Imam Mahdi.' But to this we shall return presently.

But safety was not long to be had by the Bab or by his disciples either in Shiraz or in Bushire (where the Bab then was). A fortnight afterwards twelve horsemen were sent by the governor of Fars to Bushire to arrest the Bab and bring him back to Shiraz. Such at least is one tradition,[1] but some Babis, according to Nicolas, energetically deny it. Certainly it is not improbable that the governor, who had already taken action against the Babi missionaries, should wish to observe the Bab within a nearer range, and inflict a blow on his growing popularity. Unwisely enough, the governor left the field open to the mullas, who thought by placing the pulpit of the great mosque at his disposal to be able to find material for ecclesiastical censure. But they had left one thing out of their account--the ardour of the Bab's temperament and the depth of his conviction. And so great was the impression produced by the Bab's sermon that the Shah Muhammad, who heard of it, sent a royal commissioner to study the circumstances on the spot. This step, however, was a complete failure. One may doubt indeed whether the Sayyid Yahya was ever a politician or a courtier. See below, p. 58.

The state of things had now become so threatening that a peremptory order to the governor was sent from the court to put an end to such a display of impotence. It is said that the aid of assassins was not to be refused; the death of the Bab might then be described as 'a deplorable accident.' The Bab himself was liable at any moment to be called into a conference of mullas and high state-officers, and asked absurd questions. He got tired of this and thought he would change his residence, especially as the cholera came and scattered the population. Six miserable months he had spent in Shiraz, and it was time for him to strengthen and enlighten the believers elsewhere. The goal of his present journey was Isfahan, but he was not without hopes of soon reaching Tihran and disabusing the mind of the Shah of the false notions which had become lodged in it. So, after bidding farewell to his relatives, he and his secretary and another well-tried companion turned their backs on the petty tyrant of Shiraz.[2] The Bab, however, took a very wise precaution. At the last posting station before

---

[1] *AMB*, p. 226.
[2] *AMB*, p. 370.

Isfahan he wrote to Minuchihr Khan, the governor (a Georgian by origin), announcing his approach and invoking the governor's protection.

Minuchihr Khan, who was religiously openminded though not scrupulous enough in the getting of money, [1] granted this request, and sent word to the leading mulla (the Imam-Jam'a) that he should proffer hospitality to this eminent new-comer. This the Imam did, and so respectful was he for 'forty days' that he used to bring the basin for his guest to wash his hands at mealtimes. [2] The rapidity with which the Bab indited (or revealed) a commentary on a *sura* of the Kur'an greatly impressed him, but afterwards he gave way to the persecuting tendencies of his colleagues, who had already learned to dread the presence of Babite missionaries. At the bidding of the governor, however, who had some faith in the Bab and hoped for the best, a conference was arranged between the mullas and the Bab (poor man!) at the governor's house. The result was that Minuchihr Khan declared that the mullas had by no means proved the reformer to be an impostor, but that for the sake of peace he would at once send the Bab with an escort of horsemen to the capital. This was to all appearance carried out. The streets were crowded as the band of mounted men set forth, some of the Isfahanites (especially the mullas) rejoicing, but a minority inwardly lamenting. This, however, was only a blind. The governor cunningly sent a trusty horseman with orders to overtake the travellers a short distance out of Isfahan, and bring them by nightfall to the governor's secret apartments or (as others say) to one of the royal palaces. There the Bab had still to spend a little more than four untroubled halcyon months.

But a storm-cloud came up from the sea, no bigger than a man's hand, and it spread, and the destruction wrought by it was great. On March 4, 1847, the French ambassador wrote home stating that the governor of Isfahan had died, leaving a fortune of 40 million francs. [3] He could not be expected to add what the Babite tradition affirms, that the governor offered the Bab all his riches and even the rings on his fingers,[4] to which the prophet refers in the following passage of his famous letter to Muhammad Shah, written from Maku:

---

[1] *NH*, p. 346.
[2] *Ibid*. p. 372.
[3] *AMB*, p. 242.
[4] *TN*, pp. 12, 13, 264-8; *NH*, p. 402 (Subh-i-Ezel's narrative), cp. pp. 211, 346.

'The other question is an affair of this lower world. The late Meu'timed [a title of Minuchihr Khan], one night, made all the bystanders withdraw, ... then he said to me, "I know full well that all that I have gained I have gotten by violence, and that belongs to the Lord of the Age. I give it therefore entirely to thee, for thou art the Master of Truth, and I ask thy permission to become its possessor." He even took off a ring which he had on his finger, and gave it to me. I took the ring and restored it to him, and sent him away in possession of all his goods.... I will not have a dinar of those goods, but it is for you to ordain as shall seem good to you.... [As witnesses] send for Sayyid Yahya [1] and Mulla Abdu'l-Khalik.... [2] The one became acquainted with me before the Manifestation, the other after. Both know me right well; this is why I have chosen them.' [3]

It was not likely, however, that the legal heir would waive his claim, nor yet that the Shah or his minister would be prepared with a scheme for distributing the ill-gotten riches of the governor among the poor, which was probably what the Bab himself wished. It should be added (but not, of course, from this letter) that Minuchihr Khan also offered the Bab more than 5000 horsemen and footmen of the tribes devoted to his interests, with whom he said that he would with all speed march upon the capital, to enforce the Shah's acceptance of the Bab's mission. This offer, too, the Bab rejected, observing that the diffusion of God's truth could not be effected by such means. But he was truly grateful to the governor who so often saved him from the wrath of the mullas. 'God reward him,' he would say, 'for what he did for me.'

Of the governor's legal heir and successor, Gurgin Khan, the Bab preserved a much less favourable recollection. In the same letter which has been quoted from already he says: 'Finally, Gurgin made me travel during seven nights without any of the necessaries of a journey, and with a thousand lies and a thousand acts of violence.' [4] In fact, after trying to impose upon the Bab by crooked talk, Gurgin, as soon as he found out where the Bab had taken refuge, made him start that same night, just as he was, and without bidding farewell to his newly-married wife, for the capital. 'So incensed was

---

[1] See above, p. 33.
[2] A disciple of Sheykh Ahmad. He became a Babi, but grew lukewarm in the faith (NH, pp. 231, 342 n.1).
[3] *AMB*, pp. 372, 373.
[4] *AMB*, p. 371.

he [the Bab] at this treatment that he determined to eat nothing till he arrived at Kashan [a journey of five stages], and in this resolution he persisted... till he reached the second stage, Murchi-Khur. There, however, he met Mulla Sheykh Ali... and another of his missionaries, whom he had commissioned two days previously to proceed to Tihran; and then, on learning from his guards how matters stood, succeeded in prevailing on him to take some food.' [1]

Certainly it was a notable journey, diversified by happy meetings with friends and inquirers at Kashan, Khanlik, Zanjan, Milan, and Tabriz. At Kashan the Bab saw for the first time that fervent disciple, who afterwards wrote the history of early Babism, and his equally true-hearted brother-- merchants both of them. In fact, Mirza Jani bribed the chief of the escort, to allow him for two days the felicity of entertaining God's Messenger. [2] Khanlik has also--though a mere village--its honourable record, for there the Bab was first seen by two splendid youthful heroes [3] --Riza Khan (best hated of all the Babis) and Mirza Huseyn 'Ali (better known as Baha-'ullah). At Milan (which the Bab calls 'one of the regions of Paradise'), as Mirza Jani states, 'two hundred persons believed and underwent a true and sincere conversion.' [4] and as a natural consequence we hear of many conversions.

The Bab was specially favoured in the chief of his escort, who, in the course of the journey, was fascinated by the combined majesty and gentleness of his prisoner. His name was Muhammad Beg, and his moral portrait is thus limned by Mirza Jani: 'He was a man of kindly nature and amiable character, and [became] so sincere and devoted a believer that whenever the name of His Holiness was mentioned he would incontinently burst into tears, saying,

I scarcely reckon as life the days when to me thou wert all unknown,

---

[1] *NH*, pp. 348, 349.
[2] *Ibid*. pp. 213, 214.
[3] *Ibid*. pp. 96-101.
[4] *Ibid*. p. 221. Surely these conversions were due, not to a supposed act of miraculous healing, but to the 'majesty and dignity' of God's Messenger. The people were expecting a Messiah, and here was a Personage who came up to the ideal they had formed.]What meetings took place at Zanjan and Tabriz, the early Babi historian does not report; later on, Zanjan was a focus of Babite propagandism, but just then the apostle of the Zanjan movement was summoned to Tihran. From Tabriz a remarkable cure is reported, *NH*, p. 226.

But by faithful service for what remains I may still for the past atone.'

It was the wish, both of the Bab and of this devoted servant, that the Master should be allowed to take up his residence (under surveillance) at Tabriz, where there were already many Friends of God. But such was not the will of the Shah and his vizier, who sent word to Khanlik [1] that the governor of Tabriz (Prince Bahman Mirza) should send the Bab in charge of a fresh escort to the remote mountain-fortress of Maku. The faithful Muhammad Beg made two attempts to overcome the opposition of the governor, but in vain; how, indeed, could it be otherwise? All that he could obtain was leave to entertain the Bab in his own house, where some days of rest were enjoyed. 'I wept much at his departure,' says Muhammad. No doubt the Bab often missed his respectful escort; he had made a change for the worse, and when he came to the village at the foot of the steep hill of Maku, he found the inhabitants 'ignorant and coarse.'

It may, however, be reasonably surmised that before long the Point of Wisdom changed his tone, and even thanked God for his sojourn at Maku. For though strict orders had come from the vizier that no one was to be permitted to see the Bab, any one whom the illustrious captive wished to converse with had free access to him. Most of the time which remained was occupied with writing (his secretary was with him); more than 100,000 'verses' are said to have come from that Supreme Pen.

By miracles the Bab set little store; in fact, the only supernatural gift which he much valued was that of inditing 'signs or verses, which appear to have produced a similar thrilling effect to those of the great Arabian Prophet. But in the second rank he must have valued a power to soothe and strengthen the nervous system which we may well assign to him, and we can easily believe that the lower animals were within the range of this beneficent faculty. Let me mention one of the horse-stories which have gathered round the gentle form of the Bab. [2]

It is given neither in the Babi nor in the Muslim histories of this period. But it forms a part of a good oral tradition, and it may supply the key to those

---

[1] Khanlik is situated 'about six parasangs' from Tihran (*NH*, p. 216). It is in the province of Azarbaijan.
[2] *AMB*, p. 371.

words of the Bab in his letter to Muhammad Shah:[1] 'Finally, the Sultan [i.e. the Shah] ordered that I should journey towards Maku without giving me a horse that I could ride.' We learn from the legend that an officer of the Shah did call upon the Bab to ride a horse which was too vicious for any ordinary person to mount. Whether this officer was really (as the legend states) 'Ali Khan, the warden of Maku, who wished to test the claims of 'Ali Muhammad by offering him a vicious young horse and watching to see whether 'Ali Muhammad or the horse would be victorious, is not of supreme importance. What does concern us is that many of the people believed that by a virtue which resided in the Bab it was possible for him to soothe the sensitive nerves of a horse, so that it could be ridden without injury to the rider.

There is no doubt, however, that 'Ali Khan, the warden of the fortress, was one of that multitude of persons who were so thrilled by the Bab's countenance and bearing that they were almost prompted thereby to become disciples. It is highly probable, too, that just now there was a heightening of the divine expression on that unworldly face, derived from an intensification of the inner life. In earlier times 'Ali Muhammad had avoided claiming Mahdiship (Messiahship) publicly; to the people at large he was not represented as the manifested Twelfth Imâm, but only as the Gate, or means of access to that more than human, still existent being. To disciples of a higher order 'Ali Muhammad no doubt disclosed himself as he really was, but, like a heavenly statesman, he avoided inopportune self-revelations. Now, however, the religious conditions were becoming different. Owing in some cases to the indiscretion of disciples, in others to a craving for the revolution of which the Twelfth Imâm was the traditional instrument, there was a growing popular tendency to regard Mirza 'Ali Muhammad as a 'return' of the Twelfth Imâm, who was, by force of arms, to set up the divine kingdom upon earth. It was this, indeed, which specially promoted the early Babi propagandism, and which probably came up for discussion at the Badasht conference.

In short, it had become a pressing duty to enlighten the multitude on the true objects of the Bab. Even we can see this--we who know that not much more than three years were remaining to him. The Bab, too, had probably a presentiment of his end; this was why he was so eager to avoid a continuance of the great misunderstanding. He was indeed the Twelfth Imâm,

---

[1] Ibid. pp. 249, 250.

who had returned to the world of men for a short time. But he was not a Mahdi of the Islamic type.

A constant stream of Tablets (letters) flowed from his pen. In this way he kept himself in touch with those who could not see him in the flesh. But there were many who could not rest without seeing the divine Manifestation. Pilgrims seemed never to cease; and it made the Bab still happier to receive them.

This stream of Tablets and of pilgrims could not however be exhilarating to the Shah and his Minister. They complained to the castle-warden, and bade him be a stricter gaoler, but 'Ali Khan, too, was under the spell of the Gate of Knowledge; or--as one should rather say now--the Point or Climax of Prophetic Revelation, for so the Word of Prophecy directed that he should be called. So the order went forth that 'Ali Muhammad should be transferred to another castle--that of Chihrik. [1]

At this point a digression seems necessary.

The Bab was well aware that a primary need of the new fraternity was a new Kur'an. This he produced in the shape of a book called *The Bayan* (Exposition). Unfortunately he adopted from the Muslims the unworkable idea of a sacred language, and his first contributions to the new Divine Library (for the new Kur'an ultimately became this) were in Arabic. These were a Commentary on the Sura of Yusuf (Joseph) and the Arabic Bayan. The language of these, however, was a barrier to the laity, and so the 'first believer' wrote a letter to the Bab, enforcing the necessity of making himself intelligible to all. This seems to be the true origin of the Persian Bayan.

A more difficult matter is 'Ali Muhammad's very peculiar consciousness, which reminds us of that which the Fourth Gospel ascribes to Jesus Christ. In other words, 'Ali Muhammad claims for himself the highest spiritual rank. 'As for Me,' he said, 'I am that Point from which all that exists has found existence. I am that Face of God which dieth not. I am that Light which doth not go out. He that knoweth Me is accompanied by all good; he

---

[1] Strictly, six or eight months (Feb. or April to Dec. 1847) at Maku, and two-and-a-half years at Chihrik (Dec. 1847 to July 1850).

that repulseth Me hath behind him all evil.' [1] It is also certain that in comparatively early writings, intended for stedfast disciples, 'Ali Muhammad already claims the title of Point, i.e. Point of Truth, or of Divine Wisdom, or of the Divine Mercy. [2]

It is noteworthy that just here we have a very old contact with Babylonian mythology. 'Point' is, in fact, a mythological term. It springs from an endeavour to minimize the materialism of the myth of the Divine Dwelling-place. That ancient myth asserted that the earth-mountain was the Divine Throne. Not so, said an early school of Theosophy, God, i.e. the God who has a bodily form and manifests the hidden glory, dwells on a point in the extreme north, called by the Babylonians 'the heaven of Anu.'

The Point, however, i.e. the God of the Point, may also be entitled 'The Gate,' i.e. the Avenue to God in all His various aspects. To be the Point, therefore, is also to be the Gate. 'Ali, the cousin and son-in-law of Muhammad, was not only the Gate of the City of Knowledge, but, according to words assigned to him in a *hadith*, 'the guardian of the treasures of secrets and of the purposes of God.' [3]

It is also in a book written at Maku--the Persian Bayan--that the Bab constantly refers to a subsequent far greater Person, called 'He whom God will make manifest.' Altogether the harvest of sacred literature at this mountain-fortress was a rich one. But let us now pass on with the Bab to Chihrik--a miserable spot, but not so remote as Maku (it was two days' journey from Urumiyya). As Subh-i-Ezel tells us, 'The place of his captivity was a house without windows and with a doorway of bare bricks,' and adds that 'at night they would leave him without a lamp, treating him with the utmost lack of respect.' [4] In the Persian manner the Bab himself indicated this by calling Maku 'the Open Mountain,' and Chihrik 'the Grievous Mountain.' [5] Stringent orders were issued making it difficult for friends of the Beloved Master to see him; and it may be that in the latter part of his sojourn the royal orders were more effectually carried out--a change which was possibly the result of a change in the warden. Certainly Yahya Khan

---

[1] *AMB*, p. 369.
[2] *Beyan Arabe*, p. 206.
[3] *AMB*, p. 142.
[4] *NH*, p. 403.
[5] Cp. *TN*, p. 276.

was guilty of no such coarseness as Subh-i-Ezel imputes to the warden of Chihrik. And this view is confirmed by the peculiar language of Mirza Jani, 'Yahya Khan, so long as he was warden, maintained towards him an attitude of unvarying respect and deference.'

This 'respect and deference' was largely owing to a dream which the warden had on the night before the day of the Bab's arrival. The central figure of the dream was a bright shining saint. He said in the morning that 'if, when he saw His Holiness, he found appearance and visage to correspond with what he beheld in his dream, he would be convinced that He was in truth the promised Proof.' And this came literally true. At the first glance Yahya Khan recognized in the so-called Bab the lineaments of the saint whom he had beheld in his dream. 'Involuntarily he bent down in obeisance and kissed the knee of His Holiness.'[1]

It has already been remarked that such 'transfiguration' is not wholly supernatural. Persons who have experienced those wonderful phenomena which are known as ecstatic, often exhibit what seems like a triumphant and angelic irradiation. So--to keep near home--it was among the Welsh in their last great revival. Such, too, was the brightness which, Yahya Khan and other eye-witnesses agree, suffused the Bab's countenance more than ever in this period. Many adverse things might happen, but the 'Point' of Divine Wisdom could not be torn from His moorings. In that miserable dark brick chamber He was 'in Paradise.' The horrid warfare at Sheykh Tabarsi and elsewhere, which robbed him of Babu'l Bab and of Kuddus, forced human tears from him for a time; but one who dwelt in the 'Heaven of Pre-existence' knew that 'Returns' could be counted upon, and was fully assured that the gifts and graces of Kuddus had passed into Mirza Yahya (Subh-i-Ezel). For himself he was free from anxiety. His work would be carried on by another and a greater Manifestation. He did not therefore favour schemes for his own forcible deliverance.

We have no direct evidence that Yahya Khan was dismissed from his office as a mark of the royal displeasure at his gentleness. But he must have been already removed and imprisoned,[2] when the vizier wrote to the Crown Prince (Nasiru'd-Din, afterwards Shah) and governor of Azarbaijan directing him to summon the Bab to Tabriz and convene an assembly of clergy and

---

[1] *NH*, p. 240. A slight alteration has been made to draw out the meaning.
[2] *NH*, p. 353.

laity to discuss in the Bab's presence the validity of his claims.[1] The Bab was therefore sent, and the meeting held, but there is (as Browne has shown) no trustworthy account of the deliberations. [2] Of course, the Bab had something better to do than to record the often trivial questions put to him from anything but a simple desire for truth, so that unless the great Accused had some friend to accompany him (which does not appear to have been the case) there could hardly be an authentic Babi narrative. And as for the Muslim accounts, those which we have before us do not bear the stamp of truth: they seem to be forgeries. Knowing what we do of the Bab, it is probable that he had the best of the argument, and that the doctors and functionaries who attended the meeting were unwilling to put upon record their own fiasco.

The result, however, *is* known, and it is not precisely what might have been expected, i.e. it is not a capital sentence for this troublesome person. The punishment now allotted to him was one which marked him out, most unfairly, as guilty of a common misdemeanour--some act which would rightly disgust every educated person. How, indeed, could any one adopt as his teacher one who had actually been disgraced by the infliction of stripes? [3] If the Bab had been captured in battle, bravely fighting, it might have been possible to admire him, but, as Court politicians kept on saying, he was but 'a vulgar charlatan, a timid dreamer.' [4] According to Mirza Jani, it was the Crown Prince who gave the order for stripes, but his '*farrashes* declared that they would rather throw themselves down from the roof of the palace than carry it out.' [5] Therefore the Sheykhu'l Islam charged a certain Sayyid with the 'baleful task,' by whom the Messenger of God was bastinadoed.

It seems clear, however, that there must have been a difference of opinion among the advisers of the Shah, for shortly before Shah Muhammad's death (which was impending when the Bab was in Tabriz) we are told that Prince Mahdi-Kuli dreamed that he saw the Sayyid shoot the Shah at a levee. [6]Evidently there were some Court politicians who held that the Bab

---

[1] *Ibid*. p. 284.
[2] *TN*, Note M, 'Bab Examined at Tabriz.'
[3] Cp. Isaiah liii. 5.
[4] Gobineau, p. 257.
[5] *NH*, p. 290.
[6] *Ibid*. p. 355.

was dangerous. Probably Shah Muhammad's vizier took the disparaging view mentioned above (i.e. that the Bab was a mere mystic dreamer), but Shah Muhammad's successor dismissed Mirza Akasi, and appointed Mirza Taki Khan in his place. It was Mirza Taki Khan to whom the Great Catastrophe is owing. When the Bab returned to his confinement, now really rigorous, at Chihrik, he was still under the control of the old, capricious, and now doubly anxious grand vizier, but it was not the will of Providence that this should continue much longer. A release was at hand.

It was the insurrection of Zanjan which changed the tone of the courtiers and brought near to the Bab a glorious departure. Not, be it observed, except indirectly, his theosophical novelties; the penalty of death for deviations from the True Faith had long fallen into desuetude in Persia, if indeed it had ever taken root there.[1] Only if the Kingdom of Righteousness were to be brought in by the Bab by material weapons would this heresiarch be politically dangerous; mere religious innovations did not disturb high Court functionaries. But could the political leaders any longer indulge the fancy that the Bab was a mere mystic dreamer? Such was probably the mental state of Mirza Taki Khan when he wrote from Tihran, directing the governor to summon the Bab to come once more for examination to Tabriz. The governor of Azarbaijan at this time was Prince Hamzé Mirza.

The end of the Bab's earthly Manifestation is now close upon us. He knew it himself before the event,[2] and was not displeased at the presentiment. He had already 'set his house in order,' as regards the spiritual affairs of the Babi community, which he had, if I mistake not, confided to the intuitive wisdom of Baha-'ullah. His literary executorship he now committed to the same competent hands. This is what the Baha'is History (*The Travellers Narrative*) relates,--

'Now the Sayyid Bab ... had placed his writings, and even his ring and pencase, in a specially prepared box, put the key of the box in an envelope, and sent it by means of Mulla Bakir, who was one of his first associates, to Mulla 'Abdu'l Karim of Kazwin. This trust Mulla Bakir delivered over to Mulla 'Abdu'l Karim at Kum in presence of a numerous company.... Then Mulla 'Abdu'l Karim conveyed the trust to its destination.'[3]

---

[1] Gobineau, p. 262.
[2] *NH*, pp. 235, 309-311, 418 (Subh-i-Ezel).
[3] *TN*, pp. 41, 42.

The destination was Baha-'ullah, as Mulla Bakir expressly told the 'numerous company.' It also appears that the Bab sent another letter to the same trusted personage respecting the disposal of his remains.

It is impossible not to feel that this is far more probable than the view which makes Subh-i-Ezel the custodian of the sacred writings and the arranger of a resting-place for the sacred remains. I much fear that the Ezelites have manipulated tradition in the interest of their party.

To return to our narrative. From the first no indignity was spared to the holy prisoner. With night-cap instead of seemly turban, and clad only in an under-coat,[1] he reached Tabriz. It is true, his first experience was favourable. A man of probity, the confidential friend of Prince Hamzé Mirza, the governor, summoned the Bab to a first non-ecclesiastical examination. The tone of the inquiry seems to have been quite respectful, though the accused frankly stated that he was 'that promised deliverer for whom ye have waited 1260 years, to wit the Ka'im.' Next morning, however, all this was reversed. The 'man of probity' gave way to the mullas and the populace,[2] who dragged the Bab, with every circumstance of indignity, to the houses of two or three well-known members of the clergy. 'These reviled him; but to all who questioned him he declared, without any attempt at denial, that he was the Ka'im [= he that ariseth]. At length Mulla Muhammad Mama-ghuri, one of the Sheykhi party, and sundry others, assembled together in the porch of a house belonging to one of their number, questioned him fiercely and insultingly, and when he had answered them explicitly, condemned him to death.

'So they imprisoned him who was athirst for the draught of martyrdom for three days, along with Aka Sayyid Huseyn of Yezd, the amanuensis, and Aka Sayyid Hasan, which twain were brothers, wont to pass their time for the most part in the Bab's presence....

'On the night before the day whereon was consummated the martyrdom ... he [the Bab] said to his companions, "To-morrow they will slay me shamefully. Let one of you now arise and kill me, that I may not have to endure this ignominy and shame from my enemies; for it is pleasanter to me to die by the hands of friends." His companions, with expressions of

---

[1] *NH*, p. 294.
[2] See *New History*, pp. 296 *f.*, a graphic narration.

grief and sorrow, sought to excuse themselves with the exception of Mirza Muhammad 'Ali, who at once made as though he would obey the command. His comrades, however, anxiously seized his hand, crying, "Such rash presumption ill accords with the attitude of devoted service." "This act of mine," replied he, "is not prompted by presumption, but by unstinted obedience, and desire to fulfil my Master's behest. After giving effect to the command of His Holiness, I will assuredly pour forth my life also at His feet."

'His Holiness smiled, and, applauding his faithful devotion and sincere belief, said, "To-morrow, when you are questioned, repudiate me, and renounce my doctrines, for thus is the command of God now laid upon you...." The Bab's companions agreed, with the exception of Mirza Muhammad 'Ali, who fell at the feet of His Holiness and began to entreat and implore.... So earnestly did he urge his entreaties that His Holiness, though (at first) he strove to dissuade him, at length graciously acceded.

'Now when a little while had elapsed after the rising of the sun, they brought them, without cloak or coat, and clad only in their undercoats and nightcaps, to the Government House, where they were sentenced to be shot. Aka Sayyid Huseyn, the amanuensis, and his brother, Aka Sayyid Hasan, recanted, as they had been bidden to do, and were set at liberty; and Aka Sayyid Huseyn bestowed the gems of wisdom treasured in his bosom upon such as sought for and were worthy of them, and, agreeably to his instructions, communicated certain secrets of the faith to those for whom they were intended. He (subsequently) attained to the rank of martyrdom in the Catastrophe of Tihran.

'But since Mirza Muhammad 'Ali, athirst for the draught of martyrdom, declared (himself) in the most explicit manner, they dragged him along with that (Central) Point of the Universal Circle [1] to the barrack, situated by the citadel, and, opposite to the cells on one side of the barrack, suspended him from one of the stone gutters erected under the eaves of the cells. Though his relations and friends cried, "Our son is gone mad; his confession is but the outcome of his distemper and the raving of lunacy, and it is unlawful to inflict on him the death penalty," he continued to exclaim, "I am in my right mind, perfect in service and sacrifice." .... Now he had a

---

[1] i.e. the Supreme Wisdom.

sweet young child; and they, hoping to work upon his parental love, brought the boy to him that he might renounce his faith. But he only said,--

> "Begone, and bait your snares for other quarry;
> The 'Anka's nest is hard to reach and high."

So they shot him in the presence of his Master, and laid his faithful and upright form in the dust, while his pure and victorious spirit, freed from the prison of earth and the cage of the body, soared to the branches of the Lote-tree beyond which there is no passing. [And the Bab cried out with a loud voice, "Verily thou shalt be with me in Paradise."]

'Now after this, when they had suspended His Holiness in like manner, the Shakaki regiment received orders to fire, and discharged their pieces in a single volley. But of all the shots fired none took effect, save two bullets, which respectively struck the two ropes by which His Holiness was suspended on either side, and severed them. The Bab fell to the ground, and took refuge in the adjacent room. As soon as the smoke and dust of the powder had somewhat cleared, the spectators looked for, but did not find, that Jesus of the age on the cross.

'So, notwithstanding this miraculous escape, they again suspended His Holiness, and gave orders to fire another volley. The Musulman soldiers, however, made their excuses and refused. Thereupon a Christian regiment [1] was ordered to fire the volley.... And at the third volley three bullets struck him, and that holy spirit, escaping from its gentle frame, ascended to the Supreme Horizon.' It was in July 1850.

It remained for Holy Night to hush the clamour of the crowd. The great square of Tabriz was purified from unholy sights and sounds. What, we ask, was done then to the holy bodies--that of Bab himself and that of his faithful follower? The enemies of the Bab, and even Count Gobineau, assert that the dead body of the Bab was cast out into the moat and devoured by the wild beasts. [2] We may be sure, however, that if the holy

---

[1] Why a Christian regiment? The reason is evident. Christians were outside the Babi movement, whereas the Musulman population had been profoundly affected by the preaching of the Babi, and could not be implicitly relied upon.

[2] A similar fate is asserted by tradition for the dead body of the heroic Mulla Muhammad 'Ali of Zanjan.

body were exposed at night, the loyal Babis of Tabriz would lose no time in rescuing it. The *New History* makes this statement,--

'To be brief, two nights later, when they cast the most sacred body and that of Mirza Muhammad 'Ali into the moat, and set three sentries over them, Haji Suleyman Khan and three others, having provided themselves with arms, came to the sentries and said, "We will ungrudgingly give you any sum of money you ask, if you will not oppose our carrying away these bodies; but if you attempt to hinder us, we will kill you." The sentinels, fearing for their lives, and greedy for gain, consulted, and as the price of their complaisance received a large sum of money.

'So Haji Suleyman Khan bore those holy bodies to his house, shrouded them in white silk, placed them in a chest, and, after a while, transported them to Tihran, where they remained in trust till such time as instructions for their interment in a particular spot were issued by the Sources of the will of the Eternal Beauty. Now the believers who were entrusted with the duty of transporting the holy bodies were Mulla Huseyn of Khurasan and Aka Muhammad of Isfahan,[1] and the instructions were given by Baha-'ullah.' So far our authority. Different names, however, are given by Nicolas, *AMB*, p. 381.

The account here given from the *New History* is in accordance with a letter purporting to be written by the Bab to Haji Suleyman Khan exactly six months before his martyrdom; and preserved in the *New History*, pp. 310, 311.

'Two nights after my martyrdom thou must go and, by some means or other, buy my body and the body of Mirza Muhammad 'Ali from the sentinels for 400 tumans, and keep them in thy house for six months. Afterwards lay Aka Muhammad 'Ali with his face upon my face the two (dead) bodies in a strong chest, and send it with a letter to Jenab-i-Baha (great is his majesty!). [2]Baha is, of course, the short for Baha-'ullah, and, as Prof. Browne remarks, the modest title Jenab-i-Baha was, even after the presumed date of this letter, the title commonly given to this personage.

---

[1] *TN*, p. 110, n. 3; *NH*, p. 312, n. 1.
[2] *TN*, p. 46, n. 1

The instructions, however, given by the Bab elsewhere are widely different in tendency. He directs that his remains should be placed near the shrine of Shah 'Abdu'l-'Azim, which 'is a good land, by reason of the proximity of Wahid (i.e. Subh-i-Ezel).'[1] One might naturally infer from this that Baha-'ullah's rival was the guardian of the relics of the Bab. This does not appear to have any warrant of testimony. But, according to Subh-i-Ezel himself, there was a time when he had in his hands the destiny of the bodies. He says that when the coffin (there was but one) came into his hands, he thought it unsafe to attempt a separation or discrimination of the bodies, so that they remained together 'until [both] were stolen.'

It will be seen that Subh-i-Ezel takes credit (1) for carrying out the Bab's last wishes, and (2) leaving the bodies as they were. To remove the relics to another place was tantamount to stealing. It was Baha-'ullah who ordered this removal for a good reason, viz., that the cemetery, in which the niche containing the coffin was, seemed so ruinous as to be unsafe.

There is, however, another version of Subh-i-Ezel's tradition; it has been preserved to us by Mons. Nicolas, and contains very strange statements. The Bab, it is said, ordered Subh-i-Ezel to place his dead body, if possible, in a coffin of diamonds, and to inter it opposite to Shah 'Abdu'l-'Azim, in a spot described in such a way that only the recipient of the letter could interpret it. 'So I put the mingled remains of the two bodies in a crystal coffin, diamonds being beyond me, and I interred it exactly where the Bab had directed me. The place remained secret for thirty years. The Baha'is in particular knew nothing of it, but a traitor revealed it to them. Those blasphemers disinterred the corpse and destroyed it. Or if not, and if they point out a new burying-place, really containing the crystal coffin of the body of the Bab which they have purloined, we [Ezelites] could not consider this new place of sepulture to be sacred.'

The story of the crystal coffin (really suggested by the Bayan) is too fantastic to deserve credence. But that the sacred remains had many resting-places can easily be believed; also that the place of burial remained secret for many years. Baha-'ullah, however, knew where it was, and, when circumstances favoured, transported the remains to the neighbourhood of Haifa in Palestine. The mausoleum is worthy, and numerous pilgrims from many countries resort to it.

---

[1] The spot is said to be five miles south of Tihran.

EULOGIUM ON THE MASTER

The gentle spirit of the Bab is surely high up in the cycles of eternity. Who can fail, as Prof. Browne says, to be attracted by him? 'His sorrowful and persecuted life; his purity of conduct and youth; his courage and uncomplaining patience under misfortune; his complete self-negation; the dim ideal of a better state of things which can be discerned through the obscure mystic utterances of the Bayán; but most of all his tragic death, all serve to enlist our sympathies on behalf of the young prophet of Shiraz.'

'Il sentait le besoin d'une réforme profonde à introduire dans les moeurs publiques.... Il s'est sacrifié pour l'humanité; pour elle il a donné son corps et son âme, pour elle il a subi les privations, les affronts, les injures, la torture et le martyre.' (Mons. Nicolas.)

In an old Persian song, applied to the Bab by his followers, it is written:--

In what sect is this lawful? In what religion is this lawful?
That they should kill a charmer of hearts! Why art thou a stealer of hearts?

MULLA HUSEYN OF BUSHRAWEYH

Mulla Huseyn of Bushraweyh (in the province of Mazarandan) was the embodied ideal of a Babi chief such as the primitive period of the faith produced--I mean, that he distinguished himself equally in profound theosophic speculation and in warlike prowess. This combination may seem to us strange, but Mirza Jani assures us that many students who had left cloistered ease for the sake of God and the Bab developed an unsuspected warlike energy under the pressure of persecution. And so that ardour, which in the case of the Bab was confined to the sphere of religious thought and speculation and to the unlocking of metaphorical prison-gates, was displayed in the case of Mulla Huseyn both in voyages on the ocean of Truth, and in warfare. Yes, the Mulla's fragile form might suggest the student, but he had also the precious faculty of generalship, and a happy perfection of fearlessness.

Like the Bab himself in his preparation-period, he gave his adhesion to the Sheykhi school of theology, and on the decease of the former leader (Sayyid Kazim) he went, like other members of the school, to seek for a new spiritual head. Now it so happened that Sayyid Kazim had already turned the eyes of Huseyn towards 'Ali Muhammad; already this eminent theosophist had a presentiment that wonderful things were in store for the young visitor from Shiraz. It was natural, therefore, that Huseyn should seek further information and guidance from 'Ali Muhammad himself. No trouble could be too great; the object could not be attained in a single interview, and as 'Ali Muhammad was forbidden to leave his house at Shiraz, secrecy was indispensable. Huseyn, therefore, was compelled to spend the greater part of the day in his new teacher's house.

The concentration of thought to which the constant nearness of a great prophet (and 'more than a prophet') naturally gave birth had the only possible result. All barriers were completely broken down, and Huseyn recognized in his heaven-sent teacher the Gate (*Bab*) which opened on to the secret abode of the vanished Imam, and one charged with a commission to bring into existence the world-wide Kingdom of Righteousness. To seal his approval of this thorough conversion, which was hitherto without a parallel, the Bab conferred on his new adherent the title of 'The First to Believe.'

This honourable title, however, is not the only one used by this Hero of God. Still more frequently he was called 'The Gate of the Gate,' i.e. the Introducer to Him through Whom all true wisdom comes; or, we may venture to say, the Bab's Deputy. Two other titles maybe mentioned. One is 'The Gate.' Those who regarded 'Ali Muhammad of Shiraz as the 'Point' of prophecy and the returned Imâm (the Ka'im) would naturally ascribe to his representative the vacant dignity of 'The Gate.' Indeed, it is one indication of this that the Subh-i-Ezel designates Mulla Huseyn not as the Gate's Gate, but simply as the Gate.

And now the 'good fight of faith' begins in earnest. First of all, the Bab's Deputy (or perhaps 'the Bab' [1]--but this might confuse the reader) is sent to Khurasan,[2] taking Isfahan and Tihran in his way. I need not catalogue the names of his chief converts and their places of residence. [3] Suffice it to mention here that among the converts were Baha-'ullah, Muhammad 'Ali of Zanjan, and Haji Mirza Jani, the same who has left us a much 'overworked' history of Babism (down to the time of his martyrdom). Also

---

[1] Some Babi writers (including Subh-i-Ezel) certainly call MullaHuseyn 'the Bab.'
[2] *NH*, p. 44.
[3] See Nicolas, *AMB*.

that among the places visited was Omar Khayyám's Nishapur, and that two attempts were made by the 'Gate's Gate' to carry the Evangel into the Shi'ite Holy Land (Mash-had).

But it was time to reopen communications with the 'lord from Shiraz' (the Bab). So his Deputy resolved to make for the castle of Maku, where the Bab was confined. On the Deputy's arrival the Bab foretold to him his own (the Bab's) approaching martyrdom and the cruel afflictions which were impending. At the same time the Bab directed him to return to Khurasan, adding that he should 'go thither by way of Mazandaran, for there the doctrine had not yet been rightly preached.' So the Deputy went first of all to Mazandaran, and there joined another eminent convert, best known by his Babi name Kuddus (sacred).

I pause here to notice how intimate were the relations between the two friends--the 'Gate's Gate' and 'Sacred.' Originally the former was considered distinctly the greater man. People may have reasoned somewhat thus:--It was no doubt true that Kuddus had been privileged to accompany the Bab to Mecca,[1] but was not the Bab's Deputy the more consummate master of spiritual lore? [2]

It was at any rate the latter Hero of God who (according to one tradition) opened the eyes of the majority of inquirers to the truth. It is also said that on the morning after the meeting of the friends the chief seat was occupied by Kuddus, while the Gate's Deputy stood humbly and reverentially before him. This is certainly true to the spirit of the brother-champions, one of whom was conspicuous for his humility, the other for his soaring spiritual ambition.

But let us return to the evangelistic journey. The first signs of the approach of Kuddus were a letter from him to the Bab's Deputy (the letter is commonly called 'The Eternal Witness'), together with a white robe [3] and a turban. In the letter, it was announced that he and seventy other believers would shortly win the crown of martyrdom. This may possibly be true, not only because circumstantial details were added, but because the chief leaders of the Babis do really appear to have had extraordinary spiritual

---

[1] For the divergent tradition in Nicolas, see *AMB*, p. 206.
[2] *NH*, p. 43, cp. p. 404.
[3] White was the Babite colour. See *NH*, p. 189; *TN*, p. xxxi, n. 1.

gifts, especially that of prophecy. One may ask, Did Kuddus also foresee the death of his friend? He did not tell him so in the letter, but he did direct him to leave Khurasan, in spite of the encyclical letter of the Bab, bidding believers concentrate, if possible, on Khurasan.

So, then, we see our Babi apostles and their followers, with changed route, proceeding to the province of Mazandaran, where Kuddus resided. On reaching Miyami they found about thirty believers ready to join them--the first-fruits of the preaching of the Kingdom. Unfortunately opposition was stirred up by the appearance of the apostles. There was an encounter with the populace, and the Babis were defeated. The Babis, however, went on steadily till they arrived at Badasht, much perturbed by the inauspicious news of the death of Muhammad Shah, 4th September 1848. We are told that the 'Gate's Gate' had already foretold this event,[1] which involved increased harshness in the treatment of the Bab. We cannot greatly wonder that, according to the Babis, Muhammad Shah's journey was to the infernal regions.

Another consequence of the Shah's death was the calling of the Council of Badasht. It has been suggested that the true cause of the summoning of that assembly was anxiety for the Bab, and a desire to carry him off to a place of safety. But the more accepted view--that the subject before the Council was the relation of the Babis to the Islamic laws--is also the more probable. The abrogation of those laws is expressly taught by Kurratu'l 'Ayn, according to Mirza Jani.

How many Babis took part in the Meeting? That depends on whether the ordinary Babis were welcomed to the Meeting or only the leaders. If the former were admitted, the number of Babis must have been considerable, for the 'Gate's Gate' is said to have gathered a band of 230 men, and Kuddus a band of 300, many of them men of wealth and position, and yet ready to give the supreme proof of their absolute sincerity. The notice at the end of Mirza Jani's account, which glances at the antinomian tendencies of some who attended the Meeting, seems to be in favour of a large estimate. Elsewhere Mirza Jani speaks of the 'troubles of Badasht,' at which the gallant Riza Khan performed 'most valuable services.' Nothing is said, however, of the part taken in the quieting of these troubles either by the

---

[1] *NH*, p. 45.

'Gate's Gate' or by Kuddus. Greater troubles, however, were at hand; it is the beginning of the Mazandaran insurrection (A.D. 1848-1849).

The place of most interest in this exciting episode is the fortified tomb of Sheykh Tabarsi, twelve or fourteen miles south of Barfurush. The Babis under the 'Gate's Gate' made this their headquarters, and we have abundant information, both Babite and Muslim, respecting their doings. The 'Gate's Gate' preached to them every day, and warned them that their only safety lay in detachment from the world. He also (probably as *Bab*, 'Ali Muhammad having assumed the rank of *Nukta*, Point) conferred new names (those of prophets and saints) on the worthiest of the Babis,[1] which suggests that this Hero of God had felt his way to the doctrine of the equality of the saints in the Divine Bosom. Of course, this great truth was very liable to misconstruction, just as much as when the having all things in common was perverted into the most objectionable kind of communism. [2]

'Thus,' the moralist remarks, 'did they live happily together in content and gladness, free from all grief and care, as though resignation and contentment formed a part of their very nature.'

Of course, the new names were given with a full consciousness of the inwardness of names. There was a spirit behind each new name; the revival of a name by a divine representative meant the return of the spirit. Each Babi who received the name of a prophet or an Imam knew that his life was raised to a higher plane, and that he was to restore that heavenly Being to the present age. These re-named Babis needed no other recompense than that of being used in the Cause of God. They became capable of far higher things than before, and if within a short space of time the Bab, or his Deputy, was to conquer the whole world and bring it under the beneficent yoke of the Law of God, much miraculously heightened courage would be needed. I am therefore able to accept the Muslim authority's statement. The conferring of new names was not to add fuel to human vanity, but sacramentally to heighten spiritual vitality.

Not all Babis, it is true, were capable of such insight. From the Babi account of the night-action, ordered on his arrival at Sheykh Tabarsi by Kuddus, we learn that some Babis, including those of Mazandaran, took the first

---

[1] This is a Muslim account. See *NH*, p. 303.
[2] *NH*, p. 55.

opportunity of plundering the enemy's camp. For this, the Deputy reproved them, but they persisted, and the whole army was punished (as we are told) by a wound dealt to Kuddus, which shattered one side of his face.[1] It was with reference to this that the Deputy said at last to his disfigured friend, 'I can no longer bear to look upon the wound which mars your glorious visage. Suffer me, I pray you, to lay down my life this night, that I may be delivered alike from my shame and my anxiety.' So there was another night-encounter, and the Deputy knew full well that it would be his last battle. And he 'said to one who was beside him, "Mount behind me on my horse, and when I say, 'Bear me to the Castle,' turn back with all speed." So now, overcome with faintness, he said, "Bear me to the Castle." Thereupon his companion turned the horse's head, and brought him back to the entrance of the Castle; and there he straightway yielded up his spirit to the Lord and Giver of life.' Frail of form, but a gallant soldier and an impassioned lover of God, he combined qualities and characteristics which even in the spiritual aristocracy of Persia are seldom found united in the same person.

MULLA MUHAMMAD 'ALI OF BARFURUSH

He was a man of Mazandaran, but was converted at Shiraz. He was one of the earliest to cast in his lot with God's prophet. No sooner had he beheld and conversed with the Bab, than, 'because of the purity of his heart, he at once believed without seeking further sign or proof.'[2] After the Council of Badasht he received among the Babis the title of Jenab-i-Kuddus, i.e. 'His Highness the Sacred,' by which it was meant that he was, for this age, what the sacred prophet Muhammad was to an earlier age, or, speaking loosely, that holy prophet's 're-incarnation.' It is interesting to learn that that heroic woman Kurratu'l 'Ayn was regarded as the 'reincarnation' of Fatima, daughter of the prophet Muhammad. Certainly Kuddus had enormous influence with small as well as great. Certainly, too, both he and his greatest friend had prophetic gifts and a sense of oneness with God, which go far to excuse the extravagant form of their claims, or at least the claims of others on their behalf. Extravagance of form, at any rate, lies on the surface of their titles. There must be a large element of fancy when Muhammad 'Ali of Barfurush (i.e. Kuddus) claims to be a 'return' of the great Arabian prophet and even to be the Ka'im (i.e. the Imam Mahdi), who

---

[1] *NH*, 68 *f*.
[2] *NH*, p. 39.

was expected to bring in the Kingdom of Righteousness. There is no exaggeration, however, in saying that, together with the Bab, Kuddus ranked highest (or equal to the highest) in the new community. [1]

We call him here Kuddus, i.e. holy, sacred, because this was his Babi name, and his Babi period was to him the only part of his life that was worth living. True, in his youth, he (like 'the Deputy') had Sheykhite instruction, [2] but as long as he was nourished on this imperfect food, he must have had the sense of not having yet 'attained.' He was also like his colleague 'the Deputy' in that he came to know the Bab before the young Shirazite made his Arabian pilgrimage; indeed (according to our best information), it was he who was selected by 'Ali Muhammad to accompany him to the Arabian Holy City, the 'Gate's Gate,' we may suppose, being too important as a representative of the 'Gate' to be removed from Persia. The Bab, however, who had a gift of insight, was doubtless more than satisfied with his compensation. For Kuddus had a noble soul.

The name Kuddus is somewhat difficult to account for, and yet it must be understood, because it involves a claim. It must be observed, then, first of all, that, as the early Babis believed, the last of the twelve Imams (cp. the Zoroastrian Amshaspands) still lived on invisibly (like the Jewish Messiah), and communicated with his followers by means of personages called Babs (i.e. Gates), whom the Imam had appointed as intermediaries. As the time for a new divine manifestation approached, these personages 'returned,' i.e. were virtually re-incarnated, in order to prepare mankind for the coming great epiphany. Such a 'Gate' in the Christian cycle would be John the Baptist;[3] such 'Gates' in the Muhammadan cycle would be Waraka ibn Nawfal and the other Hanifs, and in the Babi cycle Sheikh Ahmad of Ahsa, Sayyid Kazim of Resht, Muhammad 'Ali of Shiraz, and Mulla Huseyn of Bushraweyh, who was followed by his brother Muhammad Hasan. 'Ali Muhammad, however, whom we call the Bab, did not always put forward

---

[1] In *NH*, pp. 359, 399, Kuddus is represented as the 'last to enter,' and as 'the name of the last.'

[2] We may infer this from the inclusion of both persons in the list of those who went through the same spiritual exercises in the sacred city of Kufa (*NH*, p. 33).

[3] John the Baptist, to the Israelites, was the last Imam before Jesus.

exactly the same claim. Sometimes he assumed the title of Zikr [1] (i.e. Commemoration, or perhaps Reminder); sometimes (p. 81) that of Nukta, i.e. Point (= Climax of prophetic revelation). Humility may have prevented him from always assuming the highest of these titles (Nukta). He knew that there was one whose fervent energy enabled him to fight for the Cause as he himself could not. He can hardly, I think, have gone so far as to 'abdicate' in favour of Kuddus, or as to affirm with Mirza Jani [2] that 'in this (the present) cycle the original "Point" was Hazrat-i-Kuddus.' He may, however, have sanctioned Muhammad 'Ali's assumption of the title of 'Point' on some particular occasion, such as the Assembly of Badasht. It is true, Muhammad 'Ali's usual title was Kuddus, but Muhammad 'Ali himself, we know, considered this title to imply that in himself there was virtually a 'return' of the great prophet Muhammad. [3] We may also, perhaps, believe on the authority of Mirza Jani that the Bab 'refrained from writing or circulating anything during the period of the "Manifestation" of Hazrat-i-Kuddus, and only after his death claimed to be himself the Ka'im.' [4] It is further stated that, in the list of the nineteen (?) Letters of the Living, Kuddus stood next to the Bab himself, and the reader has seen how, in the defence of Tabarsi, Kuddus took precedence even of that gallant knight, known among the Babis as 'the Gate's Gate.'

On the whole, there can hardly be a doubt that Muhammad 'Ali, called Kuddus, was (as I have suggested already) the most conspicuous Babi next to the Bab himself, however hard we may find it to understand him on certain occasions indicated by Prof. Browne. He seems, for instance, to have lacked that tender sense of life characteristic of the Buddhists, and to have indulged a spiritual ambition which Jesus would not have approved. But it is unimportant to pick holes in such a genuine saint. I would rather lay stress on his unwillingness to think evil even of his worst foes. And how abominable was the return he met with! Weary of fighting, the Babis yielded themselves up to the royal troops. As Prof. Browne says, 'they were received with an apparent friendliness and even respect which served to

---

[1] And when God wills He will explain by the mediation of His Zikr (the Bab) that which has been decreed for him in the Book.--Early Letter to the Bab's uncle (*AMB*, p. 223).
[2] *NH*, p. 336.
[3] *Ibid*. p. 359.
[4] *Ibid*. p. 368.

lull them into a false security and to render easy the perfidious massacre wherein all but a few of them perished on the morrow of their surrender.'

The same historian tells us that Kuddus, loyal as ever, requested the Prince to send him to Tihran, there to undergo judgment before the Shah. The Prince was at first disposed to grant this request, thinking perhaps that to bring so notable a captive into the Royal Presence might serve to obliterate in some measure the record of those repeated failures to which his unparalleled incapacity had given rise. But when the Sa'idu'l-'Ulama heard of this plan, and saw a possibility of his hated foe escaping from his clutches, he went at once to the Prince, and strongly represented to him the danger of allowing one so eloquent and so plausible to plead his cause before the King. These arguments were backed up by an offer to pay the Prince a sum of 400 (or, as others say, of 1000) *tumans* on condition that Jenab-i-Kuddus should be surrendered unconditionally into his hands. To this arrangement the Prince, whether moved by the arguments or the *tumans* of the Sa'idu'l-'Ulama, eventually consented, and Jenab-i-Kuddus was delivered over to his inveterate enemy.

'The execution took place in the *meydan*, or public square, of Barfurush. The Sa'idu'l-'Ulama first cut off the ears of Jenab-i-Kuddus, and tortured him in other ways, and then killed him with the blow of an axe. One of the Sa'idu'l-'Ulama's disciples then severed the head from the lifeless body, and others poured naphtha over the corpse and set fire to it. The fire, however, as the Babis relate (for Subh-i-Ezel corroborates the *Parikh-i-Jadid* in this particular), refused to burn the holy remains; and so the Sa'idu'l-'Ulama gave orders that the body should be cut in pieces, and these pieces cast far and wide. This was done, but, as Haji Mirza Jani relates, certain Babis not known as such to their fellow-townsmen came at night, collected the scattered fragments, and buried them in an old ruined *madrasa* or college hard by. By this *madrasa*, as the Babi historian relates, had Jenab-i-Kuddus once passed in the company of a friend with whom he was conversing on the transitoriness of this world, and to it he had pointed to illustrate his words, saying, "This college, for instance, was once frequented, and is now deserted and neglected; a little while hence they will bury here some great man, and many will come to visit his grave, and again it will be frequented and thronged with people."' When the Baha'is are more conscious of the preciousness of their own history, this prophecy may be fulfilled, and Kuddus be duly honoured.

SAYYID YAHYA DARABI

Sayyid Yahya derived his surname Darabi from his birthplace Darab, near Shiraz. His father was Sayyid Ja'far, surnamed Kashfi, i.e. discloser (of the divine secrets). Neither father nor son, however, was resident at Darab at the period of this narrative. The father was at Buzurg, and the son, probably, at Tihran. So great was the excitement caused by the appearance of the Bab that Muhammad Shah and his minister thought it desirable to send an expert to inquire into the new Teacher's claims. They selected Sayyid Yahya, 'one of the best known of doctors and Sayyids, as well as an object of veneration and confidence,' even in the highest quarters. The mission was a failure, however, for the royal commissioner, instead of devising some practical compromise, actually went over to the Bab, in other words, gave official sanction to the innovating party. [1]

The tale is an interesting one. The Bab at first treated the commissioner rather cavalierly. A Babi theologian was told off to educate him; the Bab himself did not grant him an audience. To this Babi representative Yahya confided that he had some inclination towards Babism, and that a miracle performed by the Bab in his presence would make assurance doubly sure. To this the Babi is said to have answered, 'For such as have like us beheld a thousand marvels stranger than the fabled cleaving of the moon to demand a miracle or sign from that Perfect Truth would be as though we should seek light from a candle in the full blaze of the radiant sun.' [2] Indeed, what marvel could be greater than that of raising the spiritually dead, which the Bab and his followers were constantly performing? [3]

It was already much to have read the inspired "signs," or verses, communicated by the Bab, but how much more would it be to see his Countenance! The time came for the Sayyid's first interview with the Master. There was still, however, in his mind a remainder of the besetting sin of mullas'--arrogance,--and the Bab's answers to the questions of his guest failed to produce entire conviction. The Sayyid was almost returning home, but the most learned of the disciples bade him wait a little longer, till he too, like themselves, would see clearly. [4] The truth is that the Bab committed the

---

[1] *TN*, pp. 7, 854; Nicolas, *AMB*, pp. 233, 388.
[2] *NH*, p. 122.
[3] Accounts of miracles were spiritualized by the Bab.
[4] *NH*, p. 114.

first part of the Sayyid's conversion to his disciples. The would-be disciple had, like any novice, to be educated, and the Bab, in his first two interviews with the Sayyid, was content to observe how far this process had gone.

It was in the third interview that the two souls really met. The Sayyid had by this time found courage to put deep theological questions, and received correspondingly deep answers. The Bab then wrote on the spot a commentary on the 108th Sura of the Kur'an.[1] In this commentary what was the Sayyid's surprise to find an explanation which he had supposed to be his own original property! He now submitted entirely to the power of attraction and influence [2] exercised so constantly, when He willed, by the Master. He took the Bab for his glorious model, and obtained the martyr's crown in the second Niriz war.

MULLA MUHAMMAD 'ALI OF ZANJAN

He was a native of Mazandaran, and a disciple of a celebrated teacher at the holy city of Karbala, decorated with the title Sharifu-'l Ulama ('noblest of the Ulama'). He became a *mujtah[i]d* ('an authority on hard religious questions') at Zanjan, the capital of the small province of Khamsa, which lay between Irak and Azarbaijan. Muslim writers affirm that in his functions of *mujtahad* he displayed a restless and intolerant spirit,[3] and he himself confesses to having been 'proud and masterful.' We can, however, partly excuse one who had no congeniality with the narrow Shi'ite system prevalent in Persia. It is clear, too, that his teaching (which was that of the sect of the Akhbaris),[4] was attractive to many. He declares that two or three thousand families in Khamsa were wholly devoted to him. [5]

At the point at which this brief sketch begins, our mulla was anxiously looking out for the return of his messenger Mash-hadi Ahmad from Shiraz with authentic news of the reported Divine Manifestation. When the messenger returned he found Mulla Muhammad 'Ali in the mosque about to give a theological lecture. He handed over the letter to his Master, who, after reading it, at once turned to his disciples, and uttered these words:

---

[1] Nicolas, p. 233.
[2] *NH*, p. 115.
[3] Gobineau; Nicolas.
[4] *NH*, pp. 138, 349.
[5] *Ibid*. p. 350.

'To search for a roof after one has arrived at one's destination is a shameful thing. To search for knowledge when one is in possession of one's object is supererogatory. Close your lips [in surprise], for the Master has arisen; apprehend the news thereof. The sun which points out to us the way we should go, has appeared; the night of error and of ignorance is brought to nothing.' With a loud voice he then recited the prayer of Friday, which is to replace the daily prayer when the Imam appears.

The conversion [1] of Mulla Muhammad 'Ali had important results, though the rescue of the Bab was not permitted to be one of them. The same night on which the Bab arrived at Zanjan on his way to Tabriz and Maku, Mulla Muhammad 'Ali was secretly conveyed to Tihran. In this way one dangerous influence, much dreaded at court, was removed. And in Tihran he remained till the death of Muhammad Shah, and the accession of Nasiru'd-din Shah. The new Shah received him graciously, and expressed satisfaction that the Mulla had not left Tihran without leave. He now gave him express permission to return to Zanjan, which accordingly the Mulla lost no time in doing. The hostile mullas, however, were stirred up to jealousy because of the great popularity which Muhammad 'Ali had acquired. Such was the beginning of the famous episode of Zanjan.

KURRATU'L 'AYN

Among the Heroes of God was another glorious saint and martyr of the new society, originally called Zarrin Taj ('Golden Crown'), but afterwards better known as Kurratu'l 'Ayn ('Refreshment of the Eyes') or Jenab-i-Tahira ('Her Excellency the Pure, Immaculate'). She was the daughter of the 'sage of Kazwin,' Haji Mulla Salih, an eminent jurist, who (as we shall see) eventually married her to her cousin Mulla Muhammad. Her father-in-law and uncle was also a mulla, and also called Muhammad; he was conspicuous for his bitter hostility to the Sheykhi and the Babi sects. Kurratu'l 'Ayn herself had a flexible and progressive mind, and shrank from no theological problem, old or new. She absorbed with avidity the latest religious novelties, which were those of the Bab, and though not much sympathy could be expected from most of her family, yet there was one of her cousins who was favourable like herself to the claims of the Bab. Her father, too, though he upbraided his daughter for her wilful adhesion to

---

[1] For Muhammad 'Ali's own account, see Nicolas, *AMB*, pp. 349, 350.

'this Shiraz lad,' confessed that he had not taken offence at any claim which she advanced for herself, whether to be the Bab or *even more than that*.

Now I cannot indeed exonerate the 'sage of Kazwin' from all responsibility for connecting his daughter so closely with a bitter enemy of the Bab, but I welcome his testimony to the manifold capacities of his daughter, and his admission that there were not only extraordinary men but extraordinary women qualified even to represent God, and to lead their less gifted fellow-men or fellow-women up the heights of sanctity. The idea of a woman-Bab is so original that it almost takes one's breath away, and still more perhaps does the view--modestly veiled by the Haji--that certain men and even women are of divine nature scandalize a Western till it becomes clear that the two views are mutually complementary. Indeed, the only difference in human beings is that some realize more, and some less, or even not at all, the fact of the divine spark in their composition. Kurratu'l 'Ayn certainly did realize her divinity. On one occasion she even reproved one of her companions for not at once discerning that she was the *Kibla* towards which he ought to pray. This is no poetical conceit; it is meant as seriously as the phrase, 'the Gate,' is meant when applied to Mirza 'Ali Muhammad. We may compare it with another honorific title of this great woman--'The Mother of the World.'

The love of God and the love of man were in fact equally prominent in the character of Kurratu'l 'Ayn, and the Glorious One (el-Abha) had endowed her not only with moral but with high intellectual gifts. It was from the head of the Sheykhi sect (Haji Sayyid Kazim) that she received her best-known title, and after the Sayyid's death it was she who (see below) instructed his most advanced disciples; she herself, indeed, was more advanced than any, and was essentially, like Symeon in St. Luke's Gospel, a waiting soul. As yet, it appears, the young Shiraz Reformer had not heard of her. It was a letter which she wrote after the death of the Sayyid to Mulla Huseyn of Bushraweyh which brought her rare gifts to the knowledge of the Bab. Huseyn himself was not commissioned to offer Kurratu'l 'Ayn as a member of the new society, but the Bab 'knew what was in man,' and divined what the gifted woman was desiring. Shortly afterwards she had opportunities of perusing theological and devotional works of the Bab, by which, says Mirza Jani, 'her conversion was definitely effected.' This was at Karbala, a place beyond the limits of Persia, but dear to all Shi'ites from its associations. It appears that Kurratu'l 'Ayn had gone thither chiefly to make the acquaintance of the great Sheykhite teacher, Sayyid Kazim.

Great was the scandal of both clergy and laity when this fateful step of Kurratu'l 'Ayn became known at Kazwin. Greater still must it have been if (as Gobineau states) she actually appeared in public without a veil. Is this true? No, it is not true, said Subh-i-Ezel, when questioned on this point by Browne. Now and then, when carried away by her eloquence, she would allow the veil to slip down off her face, but she would always replace it. The tradition handed on in Baha-'ullah's family is different, and considering how close was the bond between Bahaa and Kurratu'l 'Ayn, I think it safer to follow the family of Baha, which in this case involves agreeing with Gobineau. This noble woman, therefore, has the credit of opening the catalogue of social reforms in Persia. Presently I shall have occasion to refer to this again.

Mirza Jani confirms this view. He tells us that after being converted, our heroine 'set herself to proclaim and establish the doctrine,' and that this she did 'seated behind a curtain.' We are no doubt meant to suppose that those of her hearers who were women were gathered round the lecturer behind the curtain. It was not in accordance with conventions that men and women should be instructed together, and that--horrible to say--by a woman. The governor of Karbala determined to arrest her, but, though without a passport, she made good her escape to Baghdad. There she defended her religious position before the chief mufti. The secular authorities, however, ordered her to quit Turkish territory and not return.

The road which she took was that by Kirmanshah and Hamadan (both in Irak; the latter, the humiliated representative of Ecbatana). Of course, Kurratu'l 'Ayn took the opportunity of preaching her Gospel, which was not a scheme of salvation or redemption, but 'certain subtle mysteries of the divine' to which but few had yet been privileged to listen. The names of some of her hearers are given; we are to suppose that some friendly theologians had gathered round her, partly as an escort, and partly attracted by her remarkable eloquence. Two of them we shall meet with presently in another connection. It must not, of course, be supposed that all minds were equally open. There were some who raised objections to Kurratu'l 'Ayn, and wrote a letter to the Bab, complaining of her. The Bab returned discriminating answers, the upshot of which was that her homilies were to be considered as inspired. We are told that these same objectors repented, which implies apparently that the Bab's spiritual influence was effectual at a distance.

Other converts were made at the same places, and the idea actually occurred to her that she might put the true doctrine before the Shah. It was a romantic idea (Muhammad Shah was anything thing but a devout and believing Muslim), not destined to be realized. Her father took the alarm and sent for her to come home, and, much to her credit, she gave filial obedience to his summons. It will be observed that it is the father who issues his orders; no husband is mentioned. Was it not, then, most probably on *this* return of Kurratu'l 'Ayn that the maiden was married to Mulla Muhammad, the eldest son of Haji Mulla Muhammad Taki. Mirza Jani does not mention this, but unless our heroine made two journeys to Karbala, is it not the easiest way of understanding the facts? The object of the 'sage of Kazwin' was, of course, to prevent his daughter from traversing the country as an itinerant teacher. That object was attained. I will quote from an account which claims to be from Haji Muhammad Hamami, who had been charged with this delicate mission by the family.

'I conducted Kurratu'l 'Ayn into the house of her father, to whom I rendered an account of what I had seen. Haji Mulla Taki, who was present at the interview, showed great irritation, and recommended all the servants to prevent "this woman" from going out of the house under any pretext whatsoever, and not to permit any one to visit her without his authority. Thereupon he betook himself to the traveller's room, and tried to convince her of the error in which she was entangled. He entirely failed, however, and, furious before that settled calm and earnestness, was led to curse the Bab and to load him with insults. Then Kurratu'l 'Ayn looked into his face, and said to him, "Woe unto thee, for I see thy mouth filling with blood."'

Such is the oral tradition which our informant reproduces. In criticizing it, we may admit that the gift of second sight was possessed by the Babi and Bahai leaders. But this particular anecdote respecting our heroine is (may I not say?) very improbable. To curse the Bab was not the way for an uncle to convince his erring niece. One may, with more reason, suppose that her father and uncle trusted to the effect of matrimony, and committed the transformation of the lady to her cousin Mulla Muhammad. True, this could not last long, and the murder of Taki in the mosque of Kazwin must have precipitated Kurratu'l 'Ayn's resolution to divorce her husband (as by Muhammadan law she was entitled to do) and leave home for ever. It might, however, have gone hardly with her if she had really uttered the prophecy related above. Evidently her husband, who had accused her of complicity in the crime, had not heard of it. So she was acquitted. The Bab, too, favoured the suggestion of her leaving home, and taking her place among his missionaries.[1] At the dead of night, with an escort of Babis, she set out ostensibly for Khurasan. The route which she really adopted, however, took her by the forest-country of Mazandaran, where she had the leisure necessary for pondering the religious situation.

The sequel was dramatic. After some days and nights of quietude, she suddenly made her appearance in the hamlet of Badasht, to which place a representative conference of Babis had been summoned.

The object of the conference was to correct a widespread misunderstanding. There were many who thought that the new leader came, in the most literal sense, to fulfil the Islamic Law. They realized, indeed, that the object of Muhammad was to bring about an universal kingdom of righteousness and peace, but they thought this was to be effected by wading through streams of blood, and with the help of the divine judgments. The Bab, on the other hand, though not always consistent, was moving, with some of his disciples, in the direction of moral suasion; his only weapon was 'the sword of the Spirit, which is the word of God.' When the Ka'im appeared all things would be renewed. But the Ka'im was on the point of appearing, and all that remained was to prepare for his Coming. No more should there be any distinction between higher and lower races, or between male and female. No more should the long, enveloping veil be the badge of woman's inferiority.

The gifted woman before us had her own characteristic solution of the problem. So, doubtless, had the other Babi leaders who were present, such as Kuddus and Baha-'ullah, the one against, the other in favour of social reforms.

It is said, in one form of tradition, that Kurratu'l 'Ayn herself attended the conference with a veil on. If so, she lost no time in discarding it, and broke out (we are told) into the fervid exclamation, 'I am the blast of the trumpet, I am the call of the bugle,' i.e. 'Like Gabriel, I would awaken sleeping souls.' It is said, too, that this short speech of the brave woman was followed by the recitation by Baha-'ullah of the Sura of the Resurrection (lxxv.). Such recitations often have an overpowering effect.

---

[1] Nicolas, *AMB*, p. 277.

The inner meaning of this was that mankind was about to pass into a new cosmic cycle, for which a new set of laws and customs would be indispensable.

There is also a somewhat fuller tradition. Kurratu'l 'Ayn was in Mazandaran, and so was also Baha'ullah. The latter was taken ill, and Kurratu'l 'Ayn, who was an intimate friend of his, was greatly concerned at this. For two days she saw nothing of him, and on the third sent a message to him to the effect that she could keep away no longer, but must come to see him, not, however, as hitherto, but with her head uncovered. If her friend disapproved of this, let him censure her conduct. He did not disapprove, and on the way to see him, she proclaimed herself the trumpet blast.

At any rate, it was this bold act of Kurratu'l 'Ayn which shook the foundations of a literal belief in Islamic doctrines among the Persians. It may be added that the first-fruits of Kurratu'l 'Ayn's teaching was no one less than the heroic Kuddus, and that the eloquent teacher herself owed her insight probably to Baha-'ullah. Of course, the supposition that her greatest friend might censure her is merely a delightful piece of irony. [1]

I have not yet mentioned the long address assigned to our heroine by Mirza Jani. It seems to me, in its present form, improbable, and yet the leading ideas may have been among those expressed by the prophetess. If so, she stated that the laws of the previous dispensation were abrogated, and that laws in general were only necessary till men had learnt to comprehend the Perfection of the Doctrine of the Unity. 'And should men not be able to receive the Doctrine of the Unity at the beginning of the Manifestation, ordinances and restrictions will again be prescribed for them.' It is not wonderful that the declaration of an impending abrogation of Law was misinterpreted, and converted into a licence for Antinomianism. Mirza Jani mentions, but with some reticence, the unseemly conduct of some of the Babis.

There must, however, have been some who felt the spell of the great orator, and such an one is portrayed by Mme. H. Dreyfus, in her dramatic poem *God's Heroes*, under the name of 'Ali. I will quote here a little speech

---

[1] *NH*, pp. 357-358.

of 'Ali's, and also a speech of Kurratu'l 'Ayn, because they seem to me to give a more vivid idea of the scene than is possible for a mere narrator. [1]

'ALI

'Soon we shall leave Badasht: let us leave it filled with the Gospel of life! Let our lives show what we, sincere Muhammadans, have become through our acceptance of the Bab, the Mahdi, who has awakened us to the esoteric meaning of the Resurrection Day. Let us fill the souls of men with the glory of the revealed word. Let us advance with arms extended to the stranger. Let us emancipate our women, reform our society. Let us arise out of our graves of superstition and of self, and pronounce that the Day of Judgment is at hand; then shall the whole earth respond to the quickening power of regeneration!'

QURRATU'L-'AIN

(*Deeply moved and half to herself.*)

'I feel impelled to help unveil the Truth to these men assembled. If my act be good the result will be good; if bad, may it affect me alone!

'(*Advances majestically with face unveiled, and as she walks towards Baha-'ullah's tent, addresses the men.*) That sound of the trumpet which ushers in the Day of Judgment is my call to you now! Rise, brothers! The Quran is completed, the new era has begun. Know me as your sister, and let all barriers of the past fall down before our advancing steps. We teach freedom, action, and love. That sound of the trumpet, it is I! That blast of the trumpet, it is I!

(*Exit* Qurratu'l 'Ain.)'

On the breaking up of the Council our heroine joined a large party of Babis led by her great friend Kuddus. On their arrival in Nur, however, they separated, she herself staying in that district. There she met Subh-i-Ezel, who is said to have rendered her many services. But before long the people of Mazandaran surrendered the gifted servant of truth to the Government.

---

[1] *God's Heroes*, by Laura Clifford Barney [Paris, 1909], p. 64, Act III.

We next meet with her in confinement at Tihran. There she was treated at first with the utmost gentleness, her personal charm being felt alike by her host, Mahmud the Kalantar, and by the most frigid of Persian sovereigns. The former tried hard to save her. Doubtless by using Ketman (i.e. by pretending to be a good Muslim) she might have escaped. But her view of truth was too austere for this.

So the days--the well-filled days--wore on. Her success with inquirers was marvellous; wedding-feasts were not half so bright as her religious soirées. But she herself had a bridegroom, and longed to see him. It was the attempt by a Babi on the Shah's life on August 15, 1852, which brought her nearer to the desire of her heart. One of the servants of the house has described her last evening on earth. I quote a paragraph from the account.

'While she was in prison, the marriage of the Kalantar's son took place. As was natural, all the women-folk of the great personages were invited. But although large sums had been expended on the entertainments usual at such a time, all the ladies called loudly for Kurratu'l 'Ayn. She came accordingly, and hardly had she begun to speak when the musicians and dancing-girls were dismissed, and, despite the counter attractions of sweet delicacies, the guests had no eyes and ears save for Kurratu'l 'Ayn.

'At last, a night came when something strange and sad happened. I had just waked up, and saw her go down into the courtyard. After washing from head to foot she went back into her room, where she dressed herself altogether in white. She perfumed herself, and as she did this she sang, and never had I seen her so contented and joyous as in this song. Then she turned to the women of the house, and begged them to pardon the disagreeables which might have been occasioned by her presence, and the faults which she might have committed towards them; in a word, she acted exactly like some one who is about to undertake a long journey. We were all surprised, asking ourselves what that could mean. In the evening, she wrapped herself in a *chadour*, which she fixed about her waist, making a band of her *chargud*, then she put on again her *chagchour*. Her joy as she acted thus was so strange that we burst into tears, for her goodness and inexhaustible friendliness made us love her. But she smiled on us and said, "This evening I am going to take a great, a very great journey." At this moment there was a knock at the street door. "Run and open," she said, "for they will be looking for me."

'It was the Kalantar who entered. He went in, as far as her room, and said to her, "Come, Madam, for they are asking for you." "Yes," said she, "I know it. I know, too, whither I am to be taken; I know how I shall be treated. But, ponder it well, a day will come when thy Master will give thee like treatment." Then she went out dressed as she was with the Kalantar; we had no idea whither she was being taken, and only on the following day did we learn that she was executed.'

One of the nephews of the Kalantar, who was in the police, has given an account of the closing scene, from which I quote the following:

'Four hours after sunset the Kalantar asked me if all my measures were taken, and upon the assurances which I gave him he conducted me into his house. He went in alone into the *enderun*, but soon returned, accompanied by Kurratu'l 'Ayn, and gave me a folded paper, saying to me, "You will conduct this woman to the garden of Ilkhaní, and will give her into the charge of Aziz Khan the Serdar."

'A horse was brought, and I helped Kurratu'l 'Ayn to mount. I was afraid, however, that the Babis would find out what was passing. So I threw my cloak upon her, so that she was taken for a man. With an armed escort we set out to traverse the streets. I feel sure, however, that if a rescue had been attempted my people would have run away. I heaved a sigh of relief on entering the garden. I put my prisoner in a room under the entrance, ordered my soldiers to guard the door well, and went up to the third story to find the Serdar.

'He expected me. I gave him the letter, and he asked me if no one had understood whom I had in charge. "No one," I replied, "and now that I have performed my duty, give me a receipt for my prisoner." "Not yet," he said; "you have to attend at the execution; afterwards I will give you your receipt."

'He called a handsome young Turk whom he had in his service, and tried to win him over by flatteries and a bribe. He further said, "I will look out for some good berth for you. But you must do something for me. Take this silk handkerchief, and go downstairs with this officer. He will conduct you into a room where you will find a young woman who does much harm to believers, turning their feet from the way of Muhammad. Strangle her with this handkerchief. By so doing you will render an immense service to God, and I will give you a large reward."

'The valet bowed and went out with me. I conducted him to the room where I had left my prisoner. I found her prostrate and praying. The young man approached her with the view of executing his orders. Then she raised her head, looked fixedly at him and said, "Oh, young man, it would ill beseem you to soil your hand with this murder."

'I cannot tell what passed in this young man's soul. But it is a fact that he fled like a madman. I ran too, and we came together to the serdar, to whom he declared that it was impossible for him to do what was required. "I shall lose your patronage," he said. "I am, indeed, no longer my own master; do what you will with me, but I will not touch this woman."

'Aziz Khan packed him off, and reflected for some minutes. He then sent for one of his horsemen whom, as a punishment for misconduct, he had put to serve in the kitchens. When he came in, the serdar gave him a friendly scolding: "Well, son of a dog, bandit that you are, has your punishment been a lesson to you? and will you be worthy to regain my affection? I think so. Here, take this large glass of brandy, swallow it down, and make up for going so long without it." Then he gave him a fresh handkerchief, and repeated the order which he had already given to the young Turk.

'We entered the chamber together, and immediately the man rushed upon Kurratu'l 'Ayn, and tied the handkerchief several times round her neck. Unable to breathe, she fell to the ground in a faint; he then knelt with one knee on her back, and drew the handkerchief with might and main. As his feelings were stirred and he was afraid, he did not leave her time to breathe her last. He took her up in his arms, and carried her out to a dry well, into which he threw her still alive. There was no time to lose, for daybreak was at hand. So we called some men to help us fill up the well.'

Mons. Nicolas, formerly interpreter of the French Legation at Tihran, to whom we are indebted for this narrative, adds that a pious hand planted five or six solitary trees to mark the spot where the heroine gave up this life for a better one. It is doubtful whether the ruthless modern builder has spared them.

The internal evidence in favour of this story is very strong; there is a striking verisimilitude about it. The execution of a woman to whom so much romantic interest attached cannot have been in the royal square; that would have been to court unpopularity for the Government. Moreover, there is a want of definite evidence that women were among the public victims of the 'reign of Terror' which followed the attempt on the Shah's life (cp. *TN*, p. 334). That Kurratu'l 'Ayn was put to death is certain, but this can hardly have been in public. It is true, a European doctor, quoted by Prof. Browne (*TN*, p. 313), declares that he witnessed the heroic death of the 'beautiful woman.' He seems to imply that the death was accompanied by slow tortures. But why does not this doctor give details? Is he not drawing upon his fancy? Let us not make the persecutors worse than they were.

Count Gobineau's informant appears to me too imaginative, but I will give his statements in a somewhat shortened form.

'The beauty, eloquence, and enthusiasm of Kurratu'l 'Ayn exercised a fascination even upon her gaoler. One morning, returning from the royal camp, he went into the *enderun,* and told his prisoner that he brought her good news. "I know it," she answered gaily; "you need not be at the pains to tell me." "You cannot possibly know my news," said the Kalantar; "it is a request from the Prime Minister. You will be conducted to Niyavaran, and asked, 'Kurratu'l 'Ayn, are you a Babi?' You will simply answer, 'No.' You will live alone for some time, and avoid giving people anything to talk about. The Prime Minister will keep his own opinion about you, but he will not exact more of you than this."'

The words of the prophetess came true. She was taken to Niyavaran, and publicly but gently asked, 'Are you a Babi?' She answered what she had said that she would answer in such a case. She was taken back to Tihran. Her martyrdom took place in the citadel. She was placed upon a heap of that coarse straw which is used to increase the bulk of woollen and felt carpets. But before setting fire to this, the executioners stifled her with rags, so that the flames only devoured her dead body.

An account is also given in the London manuscript of the *New History*, but as the Mirza suffered in the same persecution as the heroine, we must suppose that it was inserted by the editor. It is very short.

'For some while she was in the house of Mahmud Khan, the Kalantar, where she exhorted and counselled the women of the household, till one day she went to the bath, whence she returned in white garments, saying, "To-morrow they will kill me." Next day the executioner came and took her to the Nigaristan. As she would not suffer them to remove the veil from her face (though they repeatedly sought to do so) they applied the bow-string, and thus compassed her martyrdom. Then they cast her holy body into a well in the garden. [1]

My own impression is that a legend early began to gather round the sacred form of Her Highness the Pure. Retracing his recollections even Dr. Polak mixes up truth and fiction, and has in his mind's eye something like the scene conjured up by Count Gobineau in his description of the persecution of Tihran:--

'On vit s'avancer, entre les bourreaux, des enfants et des femmes, les chairs ouvertes sur tout le corps, avec des mèches allumées flambantes fichées dans les blessures.'

Looking back on the short career of Kurratu'l 'Ayn, one is chiefly struck by her fiery enthusiasm and by her absolute unworldliness. This world was, in fact, to her, as it was said to be to Kuddus, a mere handful of dust. She was also an eloquent speaker and experienced in the intricate measures of Persian poetry. One of her few poems which have thus far been made known is of special interest, because of the belief which it expresses in the divine-human character of some one (here called Lord), whose claims, when once adduced, would receive general recognition. Who was this Personage? It appears that Kurratu'l 'Ayn thought Him slow in bringing forward these claims. Is there any one who can be thought of but Baha-'ullah?

The Bahaite tradition confidently answers in the negative. Baha-'ullah, it declares, exercised great influence on the second stage of the heroine's development, and Kurratu'l 'Ayn was one of those who had pressed forward into the innermost sanctum of the Bab's disclosures. She was aware that 'The Splendour of God' was 'He whom God would manifest.' The words of the poem, in Prof. Browne's translation, refer, not to Ezel, but to his brother Baha-'ullah. They are in *TN*, p. 315.

---

[1] *NH*, pp. 283 *f.*

'Why lags the word, "*Am I not your Lord*"?
"*Yea, that thou art*," let us make reply.'

The poetess was a true Bahaite. More than this; the harvest sown in Islamic lands by Kurratu'l 'Ayn is now beginning to appear. A letter addressed to the *Christian Commonwealth* last June informs us that forty Turkish suffragettes are being deported from Constantinople to Akka (so long the prison of Baha-'ullah):

'"During the last few years suffrage ideas have been spreading quietly behind in the harems. The men were ignorant of it; everybody was ignorant of it; and now suddenly the floodgate is opened and the men of Constantinople have thought it necessary to resort to drastic measures. Suffrage clubs have been organized, intelligent memorials incorporating the women's demands have been drafted and circulated; women's journals and magazines have sprung up, publishing excellent articles; and public meetings were held. Then one day the members of these clubs--four hundred of them--*cast away their veils.* The staid, fossilized class of society were shocked, the good Mussulmans were alarmed, and the Government forced into action. These four hundred liberty-loving women were divided into several groups. One group composed of forty have been exiled to Akka, and will arrive in a few days. Everybody is talking about it, and it is really surprising to see how numerous are those in favour of removing the veils from the faces of the women. Many men with whom I have talked think the custom not only archaic, but thought-stifling. The Turkish authorities, thinking to extinguish this light of liberty, have greatly added to its flame, and their high-handed action has materially assisted the creation of a wider public opinion and a better understanding of this crucial problem." The other question exercising opinion in Haifa is the formation of a military and strategic quarter out of Akka, which in this is resuming its bygone importance. Six regiments of soldiers are to be quartered there. Many officers have already arrived and are hunting for houses, and as a result rents are trebled. It is interesting to reflect, as our Baha correspondent suggests, on the possible consequence of this projection of militarism into the very centre fount of the Bahai faith in universal peace.'

BAHA-'ULLAH (MIRZA HUSEYN ALI OF NUR)

According to Count Gobineau, the martyrdom of the Bab at Tabriz was followed by a Council of the Babi chiefs at Teheran (Tihran). What authority he has for this statement is unknown, but it is in itself not improbable. Formerly the members of the Two Unities must have desired to make their policy as far as possible uniform. We have already heard of the Council of Badasht (from which, however, the Bab, or, the Point, was absent); we now have to make room in our mind for the possibilities of a Council of Tihran. It was an important occasion of which Gobineau reminds us, well worthy to be marked by a Council, being nothing less than the decision of the succession to the Pontificate.

At such a Council who would as a matter of course be present? One may mention in the first instance Mirza Huseyn 'Ali, titled as Baha-'ullah, and his half-brother, Mirza Yahya, otherwise known as Subh-i-Ezel, also Jenab-i-'Azim, Jenab-i-Bazir, Mirza Asadu'llah [1] (Dayyan), Sayyid Yahya (of Darab), and others similarly honoured by the original Bab. And who were the candidates for this terribly responsible post? Several may have wished to be brought forward, but one candidate, according to the scholar mentioned, overshadowed the rest. This was Mirza Yahya (of Nur), better known as Subh-i-Ezel.

The claims of this young man were based on a nomination-document now in the possession of Prof. Browne, and have been supported by a letter given in a French version by Mons. Nicolas. Forgery, however, has played such a great part in written documents of the East that I hesitate to recognize the genuineness of this nomination. And I think it very improbable that any company of intensely earnest men should have accepted the document in preference to the evidence of their own knowledge respecting the inadequate endowments of Subh-i-Ezel.

No doubt the responsibilities of the pontificate would be shared. There would be a 'Gate' and there would be a 'Point.' The deficiencies of the 'Gate' might be made good by the 'Point.' Moreover, the 'Letters of the Living' were important personages; their advice could hardly be rejected. Still the gravity and variety of the duties devolving upon the 'Gate' and the 'Point' give us an uneasy sense that Subh-i-Ezel was not adequate to either of these posts, and cannot have been appointed to either of them by the Council. The probability is that the arrangement already made was further sanctioned, viz. that Baha-'ullah was for the present to take the private

---

[1] Gobineau, however, thinks that Mirza Asadu'llah was not present at the (assumed) Council.

direction of affairs and exercise his great gifts as a teacher, while Subh-i-Ezel (a vain young man) gave his name as ostensible head, especially with a view to outsiders and to agents of the government.

It may be this to which allusion is made in a tradition preserved by Behîah Khanum, sister of Abbas Effendi Abdul Baha, that Subh-i-Ezel claimed to be equal to his half-brother, and that he rested this claim on a vision. The implication is that Baha-'ullah was virtually the head of the Babi community, and that Subh-i-Ezel was wrapt up in dreams, and was really only a figurehead. In fact, from whatever point of view we compare the brothers (half-brothers), we are struck by the all-round competence of the elder and the incompetence of the younger. As leader, as teacher, and as writer he was alike unsurpassed. It may be mentioned in passing that, not only the *Hidden Words* and the *Seven Valleys*, but the fine though unconvincing apologetic arguments of the *Book of Ighan* flowed from Baha-'ullah's pen at the Baghdad period. But we must now make good a great omission. Let us turn back to our hero's origin and childhood.

Huseyn 'Ali was half-brother of Yahya, i.e. they had the same father but different mothers. The former was the elder, being born in A.D. 1817, whereas the latter only entered on his melancholy life in A.D. 1830.[1] Both embraced the Babi faith, and were called respectively Baha-'ullah (Splendour of God) and Subh-i-Ezel (Dawn of Eternity). Their father was known as Buzurg (or, Abbas), of the district of Nur in Mazandaran. The family was distinguished; Mirza Buzurg held a high post under government.

Like many men of his class, Mirza Huseyn 'Ali had a turn for mysticism, but combined this--like so many other mystics--with much practical ability. He became a Babi early in life, and did much to lay the foundations of the faith both in his native place and in the capital. His speech was like a 'rushing torrent,' and his clearness in exposition brought the most learned divines to his feet. Like his half-brother, he attended the important Council of Badasht, where, with God's Heroine--Kurratu'l 'Ayn--he defended the cause of progress and averted a fiasco. The Bab--'an ambassador in bonds'--he never met, but he corresponded with him, using (as it appears) the name of his half-brother as a protecting pseudonym.[2]

---

[1] It is a singular fact that an Ezelite source claims the name Baha-'ullah for Mirza Yahya. But one can hardly venture to credit this. See *TN*, p. 373 n. 1.

[2] *TN*, p. 373 n. 1.

The Bab was 'taken up into heaven' in 1850 upon which (according to a Tradition which I am compelled to reject) Subh-i-Ezel succeeded to the Supreme Headship. The appointment would have been very unsuitable, but the truth is (*pace* Gobineau) that it was never made, or rather, God did not will to put such a strain upon our faith. It was, in fact, too trying a time for any new teacher, and we can now see the wisdom of Baha-'ullah in waiting for the call of events. The Babi community was too much divided to yield a new Head a frank and loyal obedience. Many Babis rose against the government, and one even made an attempt on the Shah's life. Baha-'ullah (to use the name given to Huseyn 'Ali of Nur by the Bab) was arrested near Tihran on a charge of complicity. He was imprisoned for four months, but finally acquitted and released. No wonder that Baha-'ullah and his family were anxious to put as large a space as possible between themselves and Tihran.

Together with several Babi families, and, of course, his own nearest and dearest, Baha-'ullah set out for Baghdad. It was a terrible journey in rough mountain country and the travellers suffered greatly from exposure. On their arrival fresh misery stared the ladies in the face, unaccustomed as they were to such rough life. They were aided, however, by the devotion of some of their fellow-believers, who rendered many voluntary services; indeed, their affectionate zeal needed to be restrained, as St. Paul doubtless found in like circumstances. Baha-'ullah himself was intensely, divinely happy, and the little band of refugees--thirsty for truth--rejoiced in their untrammelled intercourse with their Teacher. Unfortunately religious dissensions began to arise. In the Babi colony at Baghdad there were some who were not thoroughly devoted to Baha-'ullah. The Teacher was rather too radical, too progressive for them. They had not been introduced to the simpler and more spiritual form of religion taught by Baha-'ullah, and probably they had had positive teaching of quite another order from some one authorized by Subh-i-Ezel.

The strife went on increasing in bitterness, until at length it became clear that either Baha-'ullah or Subh-i-Ezel must for a time vanish from the scene. For Subh-i-Ezel (or, for shortness, Ezel) to disappear would be suicidal; he knew how weak his personal claims to the pontificate really were. But Baha-'ullah's disappearance would be in the general interest; it would enable the Babis to realize how totally dependent they were, in practical matters, on Baha-'ullah. 'Accordingly, taking a change of clothes, but no money, and against the entreaties of all the family, he set out. Many months passed; he did not return, nor had we any word from him or about him.

'There was an old physician at Baghdad who had been called upon to attend the family, and who had become our friend. He sympathized much with us, and undertook on his own account to make inquiries for my father. These inquiries were long without definite result, but at length a certain traveller to whom he had described my father said that he had heard of a man answering to that description, evidently of high rank, but calling himself a dervish, living in caves in the mountains. He was, he said, reputed to be so wise and wonderful in his speech on religious things that when people heard him they would follow him; whereupon, wishing to be alone, he would change his residence to a cave in some other locality. When we heard these things, we were convinced that this dervish was in truth our beloved one. But having no means to send him any word, or to hear further of him, we were very sad.

'There was also then in Baghdad an earnest Babi, formerly a pupil of Kurratu'l 'Ayn. This man said to us that as he had no ties and did not care for his life, he desired no greater happiness than to be allowed to seek for him all loved so much, and that he would not return without him. He was, however, very poor, not being able even to provide an ass for the journey; and he was besides not very strong, and therefore not able to go on foot. We had no money for the purpose, nor anything of value by the sale of which money could be procured, with the exception of a single rug, upon which we all slept. This we sold and with the proceeds bought an ass for this friend, who thereupon set out upon the search.

'Time passed; we heard nothing, and fell into the deepest dejection and despair. Finally, four months having elapsed since our friend had departed, a message was one day received from him saying that he would bring my father home on the next day. The absence of my father had covered a little more than two years. After his return the fame which he had acquired in the mountains reached Baghdad. His followers became numerous; many of them even the fierce and untutored Arabs of Irak. He was visited also by many Babis from Persia.'

This is the account of the sister of our beloved and venerated Abdul Baha. There are, however, two other accounts which ought to be mentioned. According to the *Traveller's Narrative*, the refuge of Baha-'ullah was generally in a place called Sarkalu in the mountains of Turkish Kurdistan; more seldom he used to stay in Suleymaniyya, the headquarters of the Sunnites. Before long, however, 'the most eminent doctors of those regions got some inkling of his circumstances and conditions, and conversed with him on the solution of certain difficult questions connected with the most abstruse points of theology. In consequence of this, fragmentary accounts of this were circulated in all quarters. Several persons therefore hastened thither, and began to entreat and implore.' [1]

If this is correct, Baha-'ullah was more widely known in Turkish Kurdistan than his family was aware, and debated high questions of theology as frequently as if he were in Baghdad or at the Supreme Shrine. Nor was it only the old physician and the poor Babi disciple who were on the track of Baha-'ullah, but 'several persons'--no doubt persons of weight, who were anxious for a settlement of the points at issue in the Babi community. A further contribution is made by the Ezeli historian, who states that Subh-i-Ezel himself wrote a letter to his brother, inviting him to return. [2] One wishes that letter could be recovered. It would presumably throw much light on the relations between the brothers at this critical period.

About 1862 representations were made to the Shah that the Babi preaching at Baghdad was injurious to the true Faith in Persia. The Turkish Government, therefore, when approached on the subject by the Shah, consented to transfer the Babis from Baghdad to Constantinople. An interval of two weeks was accorded, and before this grace-time was over a great event happened--his declaration of himself to be the expected Messiah (Him whom God should manifest). As yet it was only in the presence of his son (now best known as Abdul Baha) and four other specially chosen disciples that this momentous declaration was made. There were reasons why Baha-'ullah should no longer keep his knowledge of the will of God entirely secret, and also reasons why he should not make the declaration absolutely public.

The caravan took four months to reach Constantinople. At this capital of the Muhammadan world their stay was brief, as they were 'packed off' the same year to Adrianople. Again they suffered greatly. But who would find fault with the Great Compassion for arranging it so? And who would deny

---

[1] *TN*, pp. 64, 65.
[2] *TN*, p. 359.

that there are more important events at this period which claim our interest? These are (1) the repeated attempts on the life of Baha-'ullah (or, as the Ezelis say, of Subh-i-Ezel) by the machinations of Subh-i-Ezel (or, as the Ezelis say, of Baha-'ullah), and (2) the public declaration on the part of Baha-'ullah that he, and no one else, was the Promised Manifestation of Deity.

There is some obscurity in the chronological relation of these events, i.e. as to whether the public declaration of Baha-'ullah was in definite opposition, not only to the claims of Subh-i-Ezel, but to those of Zabih, related by Mirza Jani, [1] and of others, or whether the reverse is the case. At any rate Baha-'ullah believed that his brother was an assassin and a liar. This is what he says,--'Neither was the belly of the glutton sated till that he desired to eat my flesh and drink my blood.... And herein he took counsel with one of my attendants, tempting him unto this.... But he, when he became aware that the matter had become publicly known, took the pen of falsehood, and wrote unto the people, and attributed all that he had done to my peerless and wronged Beauty.' [2]

These words are either a meaningless extravagance, or they are a deliberate assertion that Subh-i-Ezel had sought to destroy his brother, and had then circulated a written declaration that it was Baha-'ullah who had sought to destroy Subh-i-Ezel. It is, I fear, certain that Baha-'ullah is correct, and that Subh-i-Ezel did attempt to poison his brother, who was desperately ill for twenty-two days.

Another attempt on the life of the much-loved Master was prevented, it is said, by the faithfulness of the bath-servant. 'One day while in the bath Subh-i-Ezel remarked to the servant (who was a believer) that the Blessed Perfection had enemies and that in the bath he was much exposed.... Subh-i-Ezel then asked him whether, if God should lay upon him the command to do this, he would obey it. The servant understood this question, coming from Subh-i-Ezel, to be a suggestion of such a command, and was so petrified by it that he rushed screaming from the room. He first met Abbas Effendi and reported to him Subh-i-Ezel's words.... Abbas Effendi, accor-

---

[1] See *NH*, pp. 385, 394; *TN*, p. 357. The Ezelite historian includes Dayyan (see above).
[2] *TN*, pp. 368, 369.

dingly, accompanied him to my father, who listened to his story and then enjoined absolute silence upon him.' [1]

Such is the story as given by one who from her youthful age is likely to have remembered with precision. She adds that the occurrence 'was ignored by my father and brother,' and that 'our relations with Subh-i-Ezel continued to be cordial.' How extremely fine this is! It may remind us of 'Father, forgive them,' and seems to justify the title given to Baha-'ullah by his followers, 'Blessed Perfection.'

The Ezelite historian, however, gives a different version of the story. [2] According to him, it was Subh-i-Ezel whose life was threatened. 'It was arranged that Muhammad Ali the barber should cut his throat while shaving him in the bath. On the approach of the barber, however, Subh-i-Ezel divined his design, refused to allow him to come near, and, on leaving the bath, instantly took another lodging in Adrianople, and separated himself from Mirza Huseyn 'Ali and his followers.'

Evidently there was great animosity between the parties, but, in spite of the *Eight Paradises*, it appears to me that the Ezelites were chiefly in fault. Who can believe that Baha-'ullah spread abroad his brother's offences? [3] On the other hand, Subh-i-Ezel and his advisers were capable of almost anything from poisoning and assassination to the forging of spurious letters. I do not mean to say that they were by any means the first persons in Persian history to venture on these abnormal actions.

It is again Subh-i-Ezel who is responsible for the disturbance of the community.

It was represented--no doubt by this bitter foe--to the Turkish Government that Baha-'ullah and his followers were plotting against the existing order of things, and that when their efforts had been crowned with success, Baha-'ullah would be designated king.[4] This may really have been a dream of the Ezelites (we must substitute Subh-i-Ezel for Baha-'ullah); the Bahaites were of course horrified at the idea. But how should the Sultan

---

[1] Phelps, pp. 38, 39.
[2] *TN*, pp. 359, 360.
[3] *Ibid.*
[4] For another form of the story, see Phelps, *Abbas Effendi*, p. 46.

discriminate? So the punishment fell on the innocent as well as the guilty, on the Bahaites as well as the Ezelites.

The punishment was the removal of Baha-'ullah and his party and Subh-i-Ezel and his handful of followers, the former to Akka (Acre) on the coast of Syria, the latter to Famagusta in Cyprus. The Bahaites were put on board ship at Gallipoli. A full account is given by Abbas Effendi's sister of the preceding events. It gives one a most touching idea of the deep devotion attracted by the magnetic personalities of the Leader and his son.

I have used the expression 'Leader,' but in the course of his stay at Adrianople Baha-'ullah had risen to a much higher rank than that of 'Leader.' We have seen that at an earlier period of his exile Baha-'ullah had made known to five of his disciples that he was in very deed the personage whom the Bab had enigmatically promised. At that time, however, Baha-'ullah had pledged those five disciples to secrecy. But now the reasons for concealment did not exist, and Baha-'ullah saw (in 1863) that the time had come for a public declaration. This is what is stated by Abbas Effendi's sister:--[1]

'He then wrote a tablet, longer than any he had before written, [which] he directed to be read to every Babi, but first of all to Subh-i-Ezel. He assigned to one of his followers the duty of taking it to Subh-i-Ezel, reading it to him, and returning with Subh-i-Ezel's reply. When Subh-i-Ezel had heard the tablet he did not attempt to refute it; on the contrary he accepted it, and said that it was true. But he went on to maintain that he himself was co-equal with the Blessed Perfection, [2]affirming that he had a vision on the previous night in which he had received this assurance.

'When this statement of Subh-i-Ezel was reported to the Blessed Perfection, the latter directed that every Babi should be informed of it at the time when he heard his own tablet read. This was done, and much uncertainty resulted among the believers. They generally applied to the Blessed Perfection for advice, which, however, he declined to give. At length he told them that he would seclude himself from them for four months, and that during this time they must decide the question for themselves. At the end of that period, all the Babis in Adrianople, with the exception of Subh-i-

---

[1] Phelps, pp. 44-46.
[2] See p. 79.

Ezel and five or six others, came to the Blessed Perfection and declared that they accepted him as the Divine Manifestation whose coming the Bab had foretold. The Babis of Persia, Syria, Egypt, and other countries also in due time accepted the Blessed Perfection with substantial unanimity.

Baha-'ullah, then, landed in Syria not merely as the leader of the greater part of the Babis at Baghdad, but as the representative of a wellnigh perfect humanity. He did not indeed assume the title 'The Point,' but 'The Point' and 'Perfection' are equivalent terms. He was, indeed, 'Fairer than the sons of men,'[1] and no sorrow was spared to him that belonged to what the Jews and Jewish Christians called 'the pangs of the Messiah.' It is true, crucifixion does not appear among Baha-'ullah's pains, but he was at any rate within an ace of martyrdom. This is what Baha-'ullah wrote at the end of his stay at Adrianople:--[2]

'By God, my head longeth for the spears for the love of its Lord, and I never pass by a tree but my heart addresseth it [saying], 'Oh would that thou wert cut down in my name, and my body were *crucified* upon thee in the way of my Lord!'

The sorrows of his later years were largely connected with the confinement of the Bahaites at Acre (Akka). From the same source I quote the following.

'We are about to shift from this most remote place of banishment (Adrianople) unto the prison of Acre. And, according to what they say, it is assuredly the most desolate of the cities of the world, the most unsightly of them in appearance, the most detestable in climate, and the foulest in water.'

It is true, the sanitary condition of the city improved, so that Bahaites from all parts visited Akka as a holy city. Similar associations belong to Haifa, so long the residence of the saintly son of a saintly father.

If there has been any prophet in recent times, it is to Baha-'ullah that we must go. Pretenders like Subh-i-Ezel and Muhammad are quickly unmasked. Character is the final judge. Baha-'ullah was a man of the highest class--that of prophets. But he was free from the last infirmity of noble

---

[1] Ps. xlv. 2.
[2] Browne, *A Year among the Persians*, p. 518.

minds, and would certainly not have separated himself from others. He would have understood the saying, 'Would God all the Lord's people were prophets.' What he does say, however, is just as fine, 'I do not desire lordship over others; I desire all men to be even as I am.'

He spent his later years in delivering his message, and setting forth the ideals and laws of the New Jerusalem. In 1892 he passed within the veil.

BIOGRAPHICAL AND HISTORICAL (CONTINUED)

SUBH-I-EZEL (OR AZAL)

'He is a scion of one of the noble families of Persia. His father was accomplished, wealthy, and much respected, and enjoyed the high consideration of the King and nobles of Persia. His mother died when he was a child. His father thereupon entrusted him to the keeping of his honourable spouse,[1] saying, "Do you take care of this child, and see that your handmaids attend to him properly."' This 'honourable spouse' is, in the context, called 'the concubine'--apparently a second wife is meant. At any rate her son was no less honoured than if he had been the son of the chief or favourite wife; he was named Huseyn 'Ali, and his young half-brother was named Yahya.

According to Mirza Jani, the account which the history contains was given him by Mirza Huseyn 'Ali's half-brother, who represents that the later kindness of his own mother to the young child Yahya was owing to a prophetic dream which she had, and in which the Apostle of God and the King of Saintship figured as the child's protectors. Evidently this part of the narrative is imaginative, and possibly it is the work of Mirza Jani. But there is no reason to doubt that what follows is based more or less on facts derived from Mirza Huseyn 'Ali. 'I busied myself,' says the latter, 'with the instruction of [Yahya]. The signs of his natural excellence and goodness of disposition were apparent in the mirror of his being. He ever loved gravity of demeanour, silence, courtesy, and modesty, avoiding the society of other children and their behaviour. I did not, however, know that he would become the possessor of [so high] a station. He studied Persian, but made little progress in Arabic. He wrote a good *nasta'lik* hand, and was very fond of the poems of the mystics.' The facts may be decked out.

Mirza Jani himself only met Mirza Yahya once. He describes him as 'an amiable child.'[2] Certainly, we can easily suppose that he retained a childlike appearance longer than most, for he early became a mystic, and a mystic is one whose countenance is radiant with joy. This, indeed, may be

---

[1] *NH*, pp. 374 *ff*.
[2] *NH*, p. 376.

the reason why they conferred on him the name, 'Dawn of Eternity.' He never saw the Bab, but when his 'honoured brother' would read the Master's writings in a circle of friends, Mirza Yahya used to listen, and conceived a fervent love for the inspired author. At the time of the Manifestation of the Bab he was only fourteen, but very soon after, he, like his brother, took the momentous step of becoming a Babi, and resolved to obey the order of the Bab for his followers to proceed to Khurasan. So, 'having made for himself a knapsack, and got together a few necessaries,' he set out as an evangelist, 'with perfect trust in his Beloved,' somewhat as S. Teresa started from her home at Avila to evangelize the Moors. 'But when his brother was informed of this, he sent and prevented him.' [1]

Compensation, however, was not denied him. Some time after, Yahya made an expedition in company with some of his relations, making congenial friends, and helping to strengthen the Babi cause. He was now not far off the turning-point in his life.

Not long after occurred a lamentable set-back to the cause--the persecution and massacre which followed the attempt on the Shah's life by an unruly Babi in August 1852. He himself was in great danger, but felt no call to martyrdom, and set out in the disguise of a dervish [2] in the same direction as his elder brother, reaching Baghdad somewhat later. There, among the Babi refugees, he found new and old friends who adhered closely to the original type of theosophic doctrine; an increasing majority, however, were fascinated by a much more progressive teacher. The Ezelite history known as *Hasht Bihisht* ('Eight Paradises') gives the names of the chief members of the former school,[3] including Sayyid Muhammad of Isfahan, and states that, perceiving Mirza Huseyn 'Ali's innovating tendencies, they addressed to him a vigorous remonstrance.

It was, in fact, an ecclesiastical crisis, as the authors of the *Traveller's Narrative*, as well as the Ezelite historian, distinctly recognize. Baha-'ullah, too,--to give him his nobler name--endorses this view when he says, 'Then, in secret, the Sayyid of Isfahan circumvented him, and together they did that which caused a great calamity.' It was, therefore, indeed a crisis, and

---

[1] *NH*, p. 44.
[2] *TN*, p. 374.
[3] *TN*, p. 356.

the chief blame is laid on Sayyid Muhammad.[1] Subh-i-Ezel is still a mere youth and easily imposed upon; the Sayyid ought to have known better than to tempt him, for a stronger teacher was needed in this period of disorganization than the Ezelites could produce. Mirza Yahya was not up to the leadership, nor was he entitled to place himself above his much older brother, especially when he was bound by the tie of gratitude. 'Remember,' says Baha-'ullah, 'the favour of thy master, when we brought thee up during the nights and days for the service of the Religion. Fear God, and be of those who repent. Grant that thine affair is dubious unto me; is it dubious unto thyself?' How gentle is this fraternal reproof!

There is but little more to relate that has not been already told in the sketch of Baha-'ullah. He was, at any rate, harmless in Cyprus, and had no further opportunity for religious assassination. One cannot help regretting that his sun went down so stormily. I return therefore to the question of the honorific names of Mirza Yahya, after which I shall refer to the singular point of the crystal coffin and to the moral character of Subh-i-Ezel.

Among the names and titles which the Ezelite book called *Eight Paradises* declares to have been conferred by the Bab on his young disciple are Subh-i-Ezel (or Azal), Baha-'ullah, and the strange title *Mir'at* (Mirror). The two former--'Dawn of Eternity' and 'Splendour of God'--are referred to elsewhere. The third properly belongs to a class of persons inferior to the 'Letters of the Living,' and to this class Subh-i-Ezel, by his own admission, belongs. The title Mir'at, therefore, involves some limitation of Ezel's dignity, and its object apparently is to prevent Subh-i-Ezel from claiming to be 'He whom God will make manifest.' That is, the Bab in his last years had an intuition that the eternal day would not be ushered into existence by this impractical nature.

How, then, came the Bab to give Mirza Yahya such a name? Purely from cabbalistic reasons which do not concern us here. It was a mistake which only shows that the Bab was not infallible. Mirza Yahya had no great part to play in the ushering-in of the new cycle. Elsewhere the Bab is at the pains to recommend the elder of the half-brothers to attend to his junior's

---

[1] *TN*, p. 94. 'He (i.e. Sayyid Muhammad) commenced a secret intrigue, and fell to tempting Mirza Yahya, saying, "The fame of this sect hath risen high in the world; neither dread nor danger remaineth, nor is there any fear or need for caution before you."'

writing and spelling.¹ Now it was, of course, worth while to educate Mirza Yahya, whose feebleness in Arabic grammar was scandalous, but can we imagine Baha-'ullah and all the other 'letters' being passed over by the Bab in favour of such an imperfectly educated young man? The so-called 'nomination' is a bare-faced forgery.

The statement of Gobineau that Subh-i-Ezel belonged to the 'Letters of the Living' of the First Unity is untrustworthy.² M. Hippolyte Dreyfus has favoured me with a reliable list of the members of the First Unity, which I have given elsewhere, and which does not contain the name of Mirza Yahya. At the same time, the Bab may have admitted him into the second hierarchy of 18[19].³ Considering that Mirza Yahya was regarded as a 'return' of Kuddus, some preferment may conceivably have found its way to him. It was no contemptible distinction to be a member of the Second Unity, i.e. to be one of those who reflected the excellences of the older 'Letters of the Living.' As a member of the Second Unity and the accepted reflexion of Kuddus, Subh-i-Ezel may have been thought of as a director of affairs together with the obviously marked-out agent (*wali*), Baha-'ullah. We are not told, however, that Mirza Yahya assumed either the title of Bab (Gate) or that of Nukta (Point).⁴

I must confess that Subh-i-Ezel's account of the fortune of the Bab's relics appears to me, as well as to M. Nicolas,⁵ unsatisfactory and (in one point) contradictory. How, for instance, did he get possession of the relics? And, is there any independent evidence for the intermingling of the parts of the two corpses? How did he procure a crystal coffin to receive the relics? How comes it that there were Bahaites at the time of the Bab's death, and how was Subh-i-Ezel able to conceal the crystal coffin, etc., from his brother Baha-'ullah?

---

[1] The Tablets (letters) are in the British Museum collection, in four books of Ezel, who wrote the copies at Baha-'ullah's dictation. The references are--I., No. 6251, p. 162; II., No. 5111, p. 253, to which copy Rizwan Ali, son of Ezel, has appended 'The brother of the Fruit' (Ezel); III., No. 6254, p. 236; IV., No. 6257, p. 158.

[2] *Fils du Loup*, p. 156 n.3.

[3] *Fils du Loup*, p. 163 n.1. 'The eighteen Letters of Life had each a *mirror* which represented it, and which was called upon to replace it if it disappeared. There are, therefore, 18 Letters of Life and 18 Mirrors, which constituted two distinct Unities.'

[4] Others, however, give it him (*TN*, p. 353).

[5] *AMB*, p. 380 n.

Evidently Subh-i-Ezel has changed greatly since the time when both the brothers (half-brothers) were devoted, heart and soul, to the service of the Bab. It is this moral transformation which vitiates Subh-i-Ezel's assertions. Can any one doubt this? Surely the best authorities are agreed that the sense of historical truth is very deficient among the Persians. Now Subh-i-Ezel was in some respects a typical Persian; that is how I would explain his deviations from strict truth. It may be added that the detail of the crystal coffin can be accounted for. In the Arabic Bayan, among other injunctions concerning the dead,[1] it is said: 'As for your dead, inter them in crystal, or in cut and polished stones. It is possible that this may become a peace for your heart.' This precept suggested to Subh-i-Ezel his extraordinary statement.

Subh-i-Ezel had an imaginative and possibly a partly mystic nature. As a Manifestation of God he may have thought himself entitled to remove harmful people, even his own brother. He did not ask himself whether he might not be in error in attaching such importance to his own personality, and whether any vision could override plain morality. He *was* mistaken, and I hold that the Bab was mistaken in appointing (if he really did so) Subh-i-Ezel as a nominal head of the Babis when the true, although temporary vice-gerent was Baha-'ullah. For Subh-i-Ezel was a consummate failure; it is too plain that the Bab did not always, like Jesus and like the Buddha, know what was in man.

SUBSEQUENT DISCOVERIES

The historical work of the Ezelite party, called *The Eight Paradises*, makes Ezel nineteen years of age when he came forward as an expounder of religious mysteries and wrote letters to the Bab. On receiving the first letter, we are told that the Bab (or, as we should rather now call him, the Point) instantly prostrated himself in thankfulness, testifying that he was a mighty Luminary, and spoke by the Self-shining Light, by revelation. Imprisoned as he was at Maku, the Point of Knowledge could not take counsel with all his fellow-workers or disciples, but he sent the writings of this brilliant novice (if he really was so brilliant) to each of the 'Letters of the Living,' and to the chief believers, at the same time conferring on him a number of titles, including Subh-i-Ezel ('Dawn of Eternity') and Baha-'ullah ('Splendour of God ').

---

[1] *Le Beyan Arabi* (Nicolas), p. 252; similarly, p. 54.

If this statement be correct, we may plausibly hold with Professor E. G. Browne that Subh-i-Ezel (Mirza Yahya) was advanced to the rank of a 'Letter of the Living,' and even that he was nominated by the Point as his successor. It has also become much more credible that the thoughts of the Point were so much centred on Subh-i-Ezel that, as Ezelites say, twenty thousand of the words of the Bayan refer to Ezel, and that a number of precious relics of the Point were entrusted to his would-be successor.

But how can we venture to say that it is correct? Since Professor Browne wrote, much work has been done on the (real or supposed) written remains of Subh-i-Ezel, and the result has been (I think) that the literary reputation of Subh-i-Ezel is a mere bubble. It is true, the Bab himself was not masterly, but the confusion of ideas and language in Ezel's literary records beggars all comparison. A friend of mine confirms this view which I had already derived from Mirza Ali Akbar. He tells me that he has acquired a number of letters mostly purporting to be by Subh-i-Ezel. There is also, however, a letter of Baha-'ullah relative to these letters, addressed to the Muhammadan mulla, the original possessor of the letters. In this letter Baha-'ullah repeats again and again the warning: 'When you consider and reflect on these letters, you will understand who is in truth the writer.'

I greatly fear that Lord Curzon's description of Persian untruthfulness may be illustrated by the career of the Great Pretender. The Ezelites must, of course, share the blame with their leader, and not the least of their disgraceful misstatements is the assertion that the Bab assigned the name Baha-'ullah to the younger of the two half-brothers, and that Ezel had also the [non-existent] dignity of 'Second Point.'

This being so, I am strongly of opinion that so far from confirming the Ezelite view of subsequent events, the Ezelite account of Subh-i-Ezel's first appearance appreciably weakens it. Something, however, we may admit as not improbable. It may well have gratified the Bab that two representatives of an important family in Mazandaran had taken up his cause, and the character of these new adherents may have been more congenial to him than the more martial character of Kuddus.

DAYYAN

We have already been introduced to a prominent Babi, variously called Asadu'llah and Dayyan; he was also a member of the hierarchy called 'the

Letters of the Living.' He may have been a man of capacity, but I must confess that the event to which his name is specially attached indisposes me to admit that he took part in the so-called 'Council of Tihran.' To me he appears to have been one of those Babis who, even in critical periods, acted without consultation with others, and who imagined that they were absolutely infallible. Certainly he could never have promoted the claims of Subh-i-Ezel, whose defects he had learned from that personage's secretary. He was well aware that Ezel was ambitious, and he thought that he had a better claim to the supremacy himself.

It would have been wiser, however, to have consulted Baha-'ullah, and to have remembered the prophecy of the Bab, in which it was expressly foretold that Dayyan would believe on 'Him whom God would make manifest.' Subh-i-Ezel was not slow to detect the weak point in Dayyan's position, who could not be at once the Expected One and a believer in the Expected One. [1] Dayyan, however, made up as well as he could for his inconsistency. He went at last to Baha-'ullah, and discussed the matter in all its bearings with him. The result was that with great public spirit he retired in favour of Baha.

The news was soon spread abroad; it was not helpful to the cause of Ezel. Some of the Ezelites, who had read the Christian Gospels (translated by Henry Martyn), surnamed Dayyan 'the Judas Iscariot of this people.' [2] Others, instigated probably by their leaders, thought it best to nip the flower in the bud. So by Ezelite hands Dayyan was foully slain.

It was on this occasion that Ezel vented curses and abusive language on his rival. The proof is only too cogent, though the two books which contain it are not as yet printed. [3]

MIRZA HAYDAR 'ALI

A delightful Bahai disciple--the *Fra Angelico* of the brethren, as we may call him,--Mirza Haydar 'Ali was especially interesting to younger visitors to

---

[1] See Ezel's own words in *Mustaikaz*, p. 6.
[2] *TN*, p. 357.
[3] They are both in the British Museum, and are called respectively *Mustaikaz* (No. 6256) and *Asar-el-Ghulam* (No. 6256). I am indebted for facts (partly) and references to MSS. to my friend Mirza 'Ali Akbar.

Abdul Baha. One of them writes thus: 'He was a venerable, smiling old man, with long Persian robes and a spotlessly white turban. As we had travelled along, the Persian ladies had laughingly spoken of a beautiful young man, who, they were sure, would captivate me. They would make a match between us, they said.

'This now proved to be the aged Mirza, whose kindly, humorous old eyes twinkled merrily as he heard what they had prophesied, and joined in their laughter. They did not cover before him. Afterwards the ladies told me something of his history. He was imprisoned for fourteen years during the time of the persecution. At one time, when he was being transferred from one prison to another, many days' journey away, he and his fellow-prisoner, another Bahai, were carried on donkeys, head downwards, with their feet and hands secured. Haydar 'Ali laughed and sang gaily. So they beat him unmercifully, and said, "Now, will you sing?" But he answered them that he was more glad than before, since he had been given the pleasure of enduring something for the sake of God.

'He never married, and in Akka was one of the most constant and loved companions of Baha-'ullah. I remarked upon his cheerful appearance, and added, "But all you Bahais look happy." Mirza Haydar 'Ali said: "Sometimes we have surface troubles, but that cannot touch our happiness. The heart of those who belong to the Malekoot (Kingdom of God) is like the sea: when the wind is rough it troubles the surface of the water, but two metres down there is perfect calm and clearness."'

The preceding passage is by Miss E. S. Stevens (*Fortnightly Review*, June 1911). A friend, who has also been a guest in Abdul Baha's house, tells me that Haydar 'Ali is known at Akka as 'the Angel.'

ABDUL BAHA (ABBAS EFFENDI)

The eldest son of Baha-'ullah is our dear and venerated Abdul Baha ('Servant of the Splendour'), otherwise known as Abbas Effendi. He was born at the midnight following the day on which the Bab made his declaration. He was therefore eight years old, and the sister who writes her recollections five, when, in August 1852, an attempt was made on the life of the Shah by a young Babi, disaffected to the ruling dynasty. The future Abdul Baha was already conspicuous for his fearlessness and for his passionate devotion to his father. The *gamins* of Tihran (Teheran) might visit him as he paced to and fro, waiting for news from his father, but he did not mind--not he. One day his sister--a mere child--was returning home under her mother's care, and found him surrounded by a band of boys. 'He was standing in their midst as straight as an arrow--a little fellow, the youngest and smallest of the group--firmly but quietly *commanding* them not to lay their hands upon him, which, strange to say, they seemed unable to do.' [1]

This love to his father was strikingly shown during the absence of Baha-'ullah in the mountains, when this affectionate youth fell a prey to inconsolable paroxysms of grief. [2] At a later time--on the journey from Baghdad to Constantinople--Abdul Baha seemed to constitute himself the special attendant of his father. 'In order to get a little rest, he adopted the plan of riding swiftly a considerable distance ahead of the caravan, when, dismounting and causing his horse to lie down, he would throw himself on the ground and place his head on his horse's neck. So he would sleep until the cavalcade came up, when his horse would awake him by a kick, and he would remount.' [3]

In fact, in his youth he was fond of riding, and there was a time when he thought that he would like hunting, but 'when I saw them killing birds and animals, I thought that this could not be right. Then it occurred to me that better than hunting for animals, to kill them, was hunting for the souls of men to bring them to God. I then resolved that I would be a hunter of this sort. This was my first and last experience in the chase.'

'A seeker of the souls of men.' This is, indeed, a good description of both father and son. Neither the one nor the other had much of what we call technical education, but both understood how to cast a spell on the soul, awakening its dormant powers. Abdul Baha had the courage to frequent the mosques and argue with the mullas; he used to be called 'the Master' *par excellence*, and the governor of Adrianople became his friend, and proved his friendship in the difficult negotiations connected with the removal of the Bahaites to Akka. [4]

---

[1] Phelps, pp. 14, 15.
[2] Ibid. p. 20.
[3] Phelps, pp. 31, 32.
[4] Ibid. p. 20, n.2.

But no one was such a friend to the unfortunate Bahaites as Abdul Baha. The conditions under which they lived on their arrival at Akka were so unsanitary that 'every one in our company fell sick excepting my brother, my mother, an aunt, and two others of the believers.'[1] Happily Abdul Baha had in his baggage some quinine and bismuth. With these drugs, and his tireless nursing, he brought the rest through, but then collapsed himself. He was seized with dysentery, and was long in great danger. But even in this prison-city he was to find a friend. A Turkish officer had been struck by his unselfish conduct, and when he saw Abdul Baha brought so low he pleaded with the governor that a *hakîm* might be called in. This was permitted with the happiest result.

It was now the physician's turn. In visiting his patient he became so fond of him that he asked if there was nothing else he could do. Abdul Baha begged him to take a tablet (i.e. letter) to the Persian believers. Thus for two years an intercourse with the friends outside was maintained; the physician prudently concealed the tablets in the lining of his hat!

It ought to be mentioned here that the hardships of the prison-city were mitigated later. During the years 1895-1900 he was often allowed to visit Haifa. Observing this the American friends built Baha-'ullah a house in Haifa, and this led to a hardening of the conditions of his life. But upon the whole we may apply to him those ancient words:

'He maketh even his enemies to be at peace with him.'

In 1914 Abdul Baha visited Akka, living in the house of Baha-'ullah, near where his father was brought with wife and children and seventy Persian exiles forty-six years ago. But his permanent home is in Haifa, a very simple home where, however, the call for hospitality never passes unheeded. 'From sunrise often till midnight he works, in spite of broken health, never sparing himself if there is a wrong to be righted, or a suffering to be relieved. His is indeed a selfless life, and to have passed beneath its shadow is to have been won for ever to the Cause of Peace and Love.'

Since 1908 Abdul Baha has been free to travel; the political victory of the Young Turks opened the doors of Akka, as well as of other political 'houses of restraint.' America, England, France, and even Germany have shared the

---

[1] Phelps, pp. 47-51.

benefit of his presence. It may be that he spoke too much; it may be that even in England his most important work was done in personal interviews. Educationally valuable, therefore, as *Some Answered Questions* (1908) may be, we cannot attach so much importance to it as to the story--the true story--of the converted Muhammadan. When at home, Abdul Baha only discusses Western problems with visitors from the West.

The Legacy left by Baha-'ullah to his son was, it must be admitted, an onerous educational duty. It was contested by Muhammad Effendi--by means which remind us unpleasantly of Subh-i-Ezel, but unsuccessfully. Undeniably Baha-'ullah conferred on Abbas Effendi (Abdul Baha) the title of Centre of the Covenant, with the special duty annexed of the 'Expounder of the Book.' I venture to hope that this 'expounding' may not, in the future, extend to philosophic, philological, scientific, and exegetical details. Just as Jesus made mistakes about Moses and David, so may Baha-'ullah and Abdul Baha fall into error on secular problems, among which it is obvious to include Biblical and Kuranic exegesis.

It appears to me that the essence of Bahaism is not dogma, but the unification of peoples and religions in a certain high-minded and far from unpractical mysticism. I think that Abdul Baha is just as much devoted to mystic and yet practical religion as his father. In one of the reports of his talks or monologues he is introduced as saying:

'A moth loves the light though his wings are burnt. Though his wings are singed, he throws himself against the flame. He does not love the light because it has conferred some benefits upon him. Therefore he hovers round the light, though he sacrifice his wings. This is the highest degree of love. Without this abandonment, this ecstasy, love is imperfect. The Lover of God loves Him for Himself, not for his own sake.'--From 'Abbas Effendi,' by E. S. Stevens, *Fortnightly Review*, June 1911, p. 1067.

This is, surely, the essence of mysticism. As a characteristic of the Church of 'the Abha' it goes back, as we have seen, to the Bab. As a characteristic of the Brotherhood of the 'New Dispensation' it is plainly set forth by Keshab Chandra Sen. It is also Christian, and goes back to Paul and John. This is the hidden wisdom--the pearl of great price.

BIOGRAPHICAL AND HISTORICAL; AMBASSADOR TO HUMANITY

AMBASSADOR TO HUMANITY

AFTER the loss of his father the greatest trouble which befell the authorized successor was the attempt made independently by Subh-i-Ezel and the half-brother of Abdul Baha, Mirza Muhammad 'Ali, to produce a schism in the community at Akka. Some little success was obtained by the latter, who did not shrink from the manipulation of written documents. Badi-'ullah, another half-brother, was for a time seduced by these dishonest proceedings, but has since made a full confession of his error (*see Star of the West*).

It is indeed difficult to imagine how an intimate of the saintly Abdul Baha can have 'lifted up his foot' against him, the more so as Abdul Baha would never defend himself, but walked straight forward on the appointed path. That path must have differed somewhat as the years advanced. His public addresses prove that through this or that channel he had imbibed something of humanistic and even scientific culture; he was a much more complete man than St. Francis of Assisi, who despised human knowledge. It is true he interpreted any facts which he gathered in the light of revealed religious truth. But he distinctly recognized the right of scientific research, and must have had some one to guide him in the tracks of modern inquiry.

The death of his father must have made a great difference to him In the disposal of his time. It is to this second period in his life that Mr. Phelps refers when he makes this statement:

'His general order for the day is prayers and tea at sunrise, and dictating letters or "tablets," receiving visitors, and giving alms to the poor until dinner in the middle of the day. After this meal he takes a half-hour's siesta, spends the afternoon in making visits to the sick and others whom he has occasion to see about the city, and the evening in talking to the believers or in expounding, to any who wish to hear him, the Kuran, on which, even among Muslims, he is reputed to be one of the highest authorities, learned men of that faith frequently coming from great distances to consult him with regard to its interpretation.

'He then returns to his house and works until about one o'clock over his correspondence. This is enormous, and would more than occupy his entire time, did he read and reply to all his letters personally. As he finds it impossible to do this, but is nevertheless determined that they shall all receive careful and impartial attention, he has recourse to the assistance of his daughter Ruha, upon whose intelligence and conscientious devotion to the work he can rely. During the day she reads and makes digests of letters received, which she submits to him at night.'

In his charities he is absolutely impartial; his love is like the divine love--it knows no bounds of nation or creed. Most of those who benefit by his presence are of course Muslims; many true stories are current among his family and intimate friends respecting them. Thus, there is the story of the Afghan who for twenty-four years received the bounty of the good Master, and greeted him with abusive speeches. In the twenty-fifth year, however, his obstinacy broke.

Many American and English guests have been entertained in the Master's house. Sometimes even he has devoted a part of his scanty leisure to instructing them. We must remember, however, that of Bahaism as well as of true Christianity it may be said that it is not a dogmatic system, but a life. No one, so far as my observation reaches, has lived the perfect life like Abdul Baha, and he tells us himself that he is but the reflexion of Baha-'ullah. We need not, therefore, trouble ourselves unduly about the opinions of God's heroes; both father and son in the present case have consistently discouraged metaphysics and theosophy, except (I presume) for such persons as have had an innate turn for this subject.

Once more, the love of God and the love of humanity--which Abdul Baha boldly says is the love of God--is the only thing that greatly matters. And if he favours either half of humanity in preference to the other, it is women folk. He has a great repugnance to the institution of polygamy, and has persistently refused to take a second wife himself, though he has only daughters. Baha-'ullah, as we have seen, acted differently; apparently he did not consider that the Islamic peoples were quite ripe for monogamy. But surely he did not choose the better part, as the history of Bahaism sufficiently shows. At any rate, the Centre of the Covenant has now spoken with no uncertain sound.

As we have seen, the two schismatic enterprises affected the sensitive nature of the true Centre of the Covenant most painfully; one thinks of a well-known passage in a Hebrew psalm. But he was more than compensated by several most encouraging events. The first was the larger scale on which accessions took place to the body of believers; from England to the United States, from India to California, in surprising numbers, streams of enthusiastic adherents poured in. It was, however, for Russia that the high honour was reserved of the erection of the first Bahai temple. To this the Russian Government was entirely favourable, because the Bahais were strictly forbidden by Baha-'ullah and by Abdul Baha to take part in any revolutionary enterprises. The temple took some years to build, but was finished at last, and two Persian workmen deserve the chief praise for willing self-sacrifice in the building. The example thus set will soon be followed by our kinsfolk in the United States. A large and beautiful site on the shores of Lake Michigan has been acquired, and the construction will speedily be proceeded with.

It is, in fact, the outward sign of a new era. If Baha-'ullah be our guide, all religions are essentially one and the same, and all human societies are linked By a covenant of brotherhood. Of this the Bahai temples--be they few, or be they many--are the symbols. No wonder that Abdul Baha is encouraged and consoled thereby. And yet I, as a member of a great world-wide historic church, cannot help feeling that our (mostly) ancient and beautiful abbeys and cathedrals are finer symbols of union in God than any which our modern builders can provide. Our London people, without distinction of sect, find a spiritual home in St. Paul's Cathedral, though this is no part of our ancient inheritance.

Another comfort was the creation of a mausoleum (on the site of Mt. Carmel above Haifa) to receive the sacred relics of the Bab and of Baha-'ullah, and in the appointed time also of Abdul Baha.[1] This too must be not only a comfort to the Master, but an attestation for all time of the continuous development of the Modern Social Religion.

---

[1] See the description given by Thornton Chase, *In Galilee*, pp. 63 f.

It is this sense of historical continuity in which the Bahais appear to me somewhat deficient. They seem to want a calendar of saints in the manner of the Positivist calendar. Bahai teaching will then escape the danger of being not quite conscious enough of its debt to the past. For we have to reconcile not only divergent races and religions, but also antiquity and (if I may use the word) modernity. I may mention that the beloved Master has deigned to call me by a new name.[1] He will bear with me if I venture to interpret that name in a sense favourable to the claims of history.

The day is not far off when the details of Abdul Baha's missionary journeys will be admitted to be of historical importance. How gentle and wise he was, hundreds could testify from personal knowledge, and I too could perhaps say something--I will only, however, give here the outward framework of Abdul Baha's life, and of his apostolic journeys, with the help of my friend Lotfullah. I may say that it is with deference to this friend that in naming the Bahai leaders I use the capital H (He, His, Him).

Abdul Baha was born on the same night in which His Holiness the Bab declared his mission, on May 23, A.D. 1844. The Master, however, eager for the glory of the forerunner, wishes that that day (i.e. May 23) be kept sacred for the declaration of His Holiness the Bab, and has appointed another day to be kept by Bahais as the Feast of Appointment of the CENTRE OF THE COVENANT--Nov. 26. It should be mentioned that the great office and dignity of Centre of the Covenant was conferred on Abdul Baha Abbas Effendi by His father.

It will be in the memory of most that the Master was retained a prisoner under the Turkish Government at Akka until Sept. 1908, when the doors of His prison were opened by the Young Turks. After this He stayed in Akka and Haifa for some time, and then went to Egypt, where He sojourned for about two years. He then began His great European journey. He first visited London. On His way thither He spent some few weeks in Geneva. [2] On Monday, Sept. 3, 1911, He arrived in London; the great city was honoured by a visit of twenty-six days. During His stay in London He made a visit one afternoon to Vanners' in Byfleet on Sept. 9, where He spoke to a number of working women.

---

[1] 'Spiritual Philosopher.'

[2] Mr. H. Holley has given a classic description of Abdul Baha, whom he met at Thonon on the shores of Lake Leman, in his *Modern Social Religion*, Appendix I.

He also made a week-end visit to Clifton (Bristol) from Sept. 23, 1911, to Sept. 25.

On Sept. 29, 1911, He started from London and went to Paris and stayed there for about two months, and from there He went to Alexandria.

His second journey consumed much time, but the fragrance of God accompanied Him. On March 25, 1912, He embarked from Alexandria for America. He made a long tour in almost all the more important cities of the United States and Canada.

On Saturday, Dec. 14, 1912, the Master--Abdul Baha--arrived in Liverpool from New York. He stayed there for two days. On the following Monday, Dec. 16, 1912, He arrived in London. There He stayed till Jan. 21, 1913, when His Holiness went to Paris.

During His stay in London He visited Oxford (where He and His party--of Persians mainly--were the guests of Professor and Mrs. Cheyne), Edinburgh, Clifton, and Woking. It is fitting to notice here that the audience at Oxford, though highly academic, seemed to be deeply interested, and that Dr. Carpenter made an admirable speech.

On Jan. 6, 1913, Abdul Baha went to Edinburgh, and stayed at Mrs. Alexander Whyte's. In the course of these three days He addressed the Theosophical Society, the Esperanto Society, and many of the students, including representatives of almost all parts of the East. He also spoke to two or three other large meetings in the bleak but receptive 'northern Athens.' It is pleasant to add that here, as elsewhere, many seekers came and had private interviews with Him. It was a fruitful season, and He then returned to London.

On Wednesday, Jan. 15, 1912, He paid another visit to Clifton, and in the evening spoke to a large gathering at 8.30 P.M. at Clifton Guest House. On the following day He returned to London.

On Friday, Jan. 17, Abdul Baha went to the Muhammadan Mosque at Woking. There, in the Muhammadan Mosque He spoke to a large audience of Muhammadans and Christians who gathered there from different parts of the world.

On Jan. 21, 1913, this glorious time had an end. He started by express train for Paris from Victoria Station. He stayed at the French capital till the middle of June, addressing (by the help of His interpreter) 'all sorts and conditions of men.' Once more Paris proved how thoroughly it deserved the title of 'city of ideas.' During this time He visited Stuttgart, Budapest, and Vienna. At Budapest He had the great pleasure of meeting Arminius Vambery, who had become virtually a strong adherent of the cause.

Will the Master be able to visit India? He has said Himself that some magnetic personality might draw Him. Will the Brahmaists be pleased to see Him? At any rate, our beloved Master has the requisite tact. Could Indians and English be really united except by the help of the Bahais? The following Tablet (Epistle) was addressed by the Master to the Bahais in London, who had sent Him a New Year's greeting on March 21, 1914:--

'HE IS GOD!

'O shining Bahais! Your New Year's greeting brought infinite joy and fragrance, and became the cause of our daily rejoicing and gladness.

'Thanks be to God! that in that city which is often dark because of cloud, mist, and smoke, such bright candles (as you) are glowing, whose emanating light is God's guidance, and whose influencing warmth is as the burning Fire of the Love of God.

'This your social gathering on the Great Feast is like unto a Mother who will in future beget many Heavenly Feasts. So that all eyes may be amazed as to what effulgence the true Sun of the East has shed on the West.

'How It has changed the Occidentals into Orientals, and illumined the Western Horizon with the Luminary of the East!

'Then, in thanksgiving for this great gift, favour, and grace, rejoice ye and be exceeding glad, and engage ye in praising and sanctifying the Lord of Hosts.

'Hearken to the song of the Highest Concourse, and by the melody of Abha's Kingdom lift ye up the cry of "Ya Baha-'ul-Abha!"

'So that Abdul Baha and all the Eastern Bahais may give themselves to praise of the Loving Lord, and cry aloud, "Most Pure and Holy is the Lord, Who has changed the West into the East with lights of Guidance!"

'Upon you all be the Glory of the Most Glorious One!'

Alas! the brightness of the day has been darkened for the Bahai Brotherhood all over the world. Words fail me for the adequate expression of my sorrow at the adjournment of the hope of Peace. Yet the idea has been expressed, and cannot return to the Thinker void of results. The estrangement of races and religions is only the fruit of ignorance, and their reconciliation is only a question of time. *Sursum corda.*

A SERIES OF ILLUSTRATIVE STUDIES BEARING ON COMPARATIVE RELIGION

EIGHTEEN (OR, WITH THE BAB, NINETEEN) LETTERS OF THE LIVING OF THE FIRST UNITY

THE Letters of the Living were the most faithful and most gifted of the disciples of the so-called Gate or Point. See *Traveller's Narrative*, Introd. p. xvi.

Babu'l Bab.
A. Muhammad Hasan, his brother.
A. Muhammad Baghir, his nephew.
A. Mulla Ali Bustani.
Janabe Mulla Khodabacksh Qutshani.
Janabe Hasan Bajastani.
Janabe A. Sayyid Hussain Yardi.
Janabe Mirza Muhammad Ruzi Khan.
Janabe Sayyïd Hindi.
Janabe Mulla Mahmud Khoyï.
Janabe Mulla Jalil Urumiyi.
Janabe Mulla Muhammad Abdul Maraghaï.
Janabe Mulla Baghir Tabrizi.
Janabe Mulla Yusif Ardabili.
Mirza Hadi, son of Mirza Abdu'l Wahab Qazwini.
Janabe Mirza Muhammad 'Ali Qazwini.
Janabi Tahirah.
Hazrati Quddus.

TITLES OF THE BAB, ETC.

There is a puzzling variation in the claims of 'Ali Muhammad. Originally he represented himself as the Gate of the City of Knowledge, or--which is virtually the same thing--as the Gate leading to the invisible twelfth Imâm who was also regarded as the Essence of Divine Wisdom. It was this Imâm who was destined as Ka'im (he who is to arise) to bring the whole world by force into subjection to the true God. Now there was one person who was obviously far better suited than 'Ali Muhammad (the Bab) to carry out the programme for the Ka'im, and that was Hazrat-i'-Kuddus (to whom I have devoted a separate section). For some time, therefore, before the death of Kuddus, 'Ali Muhammad abstained from writing or speaking *ex cathedra*, as the returned Ka'im; he was probably called 'the Point.' After the death of this heroic personage, however, he undoubtedly resumed his previous position.

On this matter Mr. Leslie Johnston remarks that the alternation of the two characters in the same person is as foreign to Christ's thought as it is essential to the Bab's. [1] This is perfectly true. The divine-human Being called the Messiah has assumed human form; the only development of which he is capable is self-realization. The Imamate is little more than a function, but the Messiahship is held by a person, not as a mere function, but as a part of his nature. This is not an unfair criticism. The alternation seems to me, as well as to Mr. Johnston, psychologically impossible. But all the more importance attaches to the sublime figure of Baha-'ullah, who realized his oneness with God, and whose forerunner is like unto him (the Bab).

The following utterance of the Bab is deserving of consideration:

'Then, verily, if God manifested one like thee, he would inherit the cause from God, the One, the Unique. But if he doth not appear, then know that verily God hath not willed that he should make himself known. Leave the cause, then, to him, the educator of you all, and of the whole world.'

The reference to Baha-'ullah is unmistakable. He is 'one like thee,' i.e. Ezel's near kinsman, and is a consummate educator, and God's Manifestation.

Another point is also important. The Bab expressed a wish that his widow should not marry again. Subh-i-Ezel, however, who was not, even in theory, a monogamist, lost no time in taking the lady for a wife. He cannot have been the Bab's successor.

LETTER OF ONE EXPECTING MARTYRDOM[2]

---

[1] *Some Alternatives to Jesus Christ*, p. 117.
[2] The letter is addressed to a brother.

'He is the Compassionate [*superscription*]. O thou who art my Kibla! My condition, thanks to God, has no fault, and "to every difficulty succeedeth ease." You have written that this matter has no end. What matter, then, has any end? We, at least, have no discontent in this matter; nay, rather we are unable sufficiently to express our thanks for this favour. The end of this matter is to be slain in the way of God, and O! what happiness is this! The will of God will come to pass with regard to His servants, neither can human plans avert the Divine decree. What God wishes comes to pass, and there is no power and no strength, but in God. O thou who art my Kibla! the end of the world is death: "every soul tastes of death." If the appointed fate which God (mighty and glorious is He) hath decreed overtake me, then God is the guardian of my family, and thou art mine executor: behave in such wise as is pleasing to God, and pardon whatever has proceeded from me which may seem lacking in courtesy, or contrary to the respect due from juniors: and seek pardon for me from all those of my household, and commit me to God. God is my portion, and how good is He as a guardian!'

THE BAHAI VIEW OF RELIGION

The practical purpose of the Revelation of Baha-'ullah is thus described on authority:

To unite all the races of the world in perfect harmony, which can only be done, in my opinion, on a religious basis.

Warfare must be abolished, and international difficulties be settled by a Council of Arbitration. This may require further consideration.

It is commanded that every one should practise some trade, art, or profession. Work done in a faithful spirit of service is accepted as an act of worship.

Mendicity is strictly forbidden, but work must be provided for all. A brilliant anticipation!

There is to be no priesthood apart from the laity. Early Christianity and Buddhism both ratify this. Teachers and investigators would, of course, always be wanted.

The practice of Asceticism, living the hermit life or in secluded communities, is prohibited.

Monogamy is enjoined. Baha-'ullah, no doubt, had two wives. This was 'for the hardness of men's hearts'; he desired the spread of monogamy.

Education for all, boys and girls equally, is commanded as a religious duty-- the childless should educate a child.

The equality of men and women is asserted.

A universal language as a means of international communication is to be formed. Abdul Baha is much in favour of *Esperanto*, the noble inventor of which sets all other inventors a worthy example of unselfishness.

Gambling, the use of alcoholic liquors as a beverage, the taking of opium, cruelty to animals and slavery, are forbidden.

A certain portion of a man's income must be devoted to charity. The administration of charitable funds, the provision for widows and for the sick and disabled, the education and care of orphans, will be arranged and managed by elected Councils.

THE NEW DISPENSATION

The contrast between the Old and the New is well exemplified in the contrasting lives of Rammohan Roy, Debendranath Tagore, and Keshab Chandra Sen. As an Indian writer says: 'The sweep of the New Dispensation is broader than the Brahmo Samaj. The whole religious world is in the grasp of a great purpose which, in its fresh unfolding of the new age, we call the New Dispensation. The New Dispensation is not a local phenomenon; it is not confined to Calcutta or to India; our Brotherhood is but one body whose thought it functions to-day; it is not topographical, it is operative in all the world-religions.' [1]

'No full account has yet been given to the New Brotherhood's work and experiences during that period. Men of various ranks came, drawn

---

[1] Cp. Auguste Sabatier on the *Religion of the Spirit*, and Mozoomdar's work on the same subject.

together by the magnetic personality of the man they loved, knowing he loved them all with a larger love; his leadership was one of love, and they caught the contagion of his conviction.... And so, if I were to write at length, I could cite one illustration after another of transformed lives--lives charged with a new spirit shown in the work achieved, the sufferings borne, the persecutions accepted, deep spiritual gladness experienced in the midst of pain, the fellowship with God realized day after day' (Benoyendra Nath Sen, *The Spirit of the New Dispensation*). The test of a religion is its capacity for producing noble men and women.

MANIFESTATION

God Himself in His inmost essence cannot be either imagined or comprehended, cannot be named. But in some measure He can be known by His Manifestations, chief among whom is that Heavenly Being known variously as Michael, the Son of man, the Logos, and Sofia. These names are only concessions to the weakness of the people. This Heavenly Being is sometimes spoken of allusively as the Face or Name, the Gate and the Point (of Knowledge). See p. 101.

The Manifestations may also be called Manifesters or Revealers. They make God known to the human folk so far as this can be done by Mirrors, and especially (as Tagore has most beautifully shown) in His inexhaustible love. They need not have the learning of the schools. They would mistake their office if they ever interfered with discoveries or problems of criticism or of science.

The Bab announced that he himself owed nothing to any earthly teacher. A heavenly teacher, however, if he touched the subject, would surely have taught the Bab better Arabic. It is a psychological problem how the Bab can lay so much stress on his 'signs' (ayât) or verses as decisive of the claims of a prophet. One is tempted to surmise that in the Bab's Arabic work there has been collaboration.

What constitutes 'signs' or verses? Prof. Browne gives this answer: [1] 'Eloquence of diction, rapidity of utterance, knowledge unacquired by study, claim to divine origin, power to affect and control the minds of men.' I do not myself see how the possession of an Arabic which some people

---

[1] E. G. Browne, *JRAS*, 1889, p. 155.

think very poor and others put down to the help of an amanuensis, can be brought within the range of Messianic lore. It is spiritual truth that we look for from the Bab. Secular wisdom, including the knowledge of languages, we turn over to the company of trained scholars.

Spiritual truth, then, is the domain of the prophets of Bahaism. A prophet who steps aside from the region in which he is at home is fallible like other men. Even in the sphere of exposition of sacred texts the greatest of prophets is liable to err. In this way I am bound to say that Baha-'ullah himself has made mistakes, and can we be surprised that the almost equally venerated Abdul Baha has made many slips? It is necessary to make this pronouncement, lest possible friends should be converted into seeming enemies. The claim of infallibility has done harm enough already in the Roman Church!

Baha-'ullah may no doubt be invoked on the other side. This is the absolutely correct statement of his son Abdul Baha. 'He (Baha-'ullah) entered into a Covenant and Testament with the people. He appointed a Centre of the Covenant, He wrote with his own pen ... appointing him the Expounder of the Book.' [1] But Baha-'ullah is as little to be followed on questions of philology as Jesus Christ, who is not a manifester of science but of heavenly lore. The question of Sinlessness I postpone.

GREAT MANIFESTATION; WHEN?

I do not myself think that the interval of nineteen years for the Great Manifestation was meant by the Bab to be taken literally. The number 19 may be merely a conventional sacred number and have no historical significance. I am therefore not to be shaken by a reference to these words of the Bab, quoted in substance by Mirza Abu'l Fazl, that after nine years all good will come to his followers, or by the Mirza's comment that it was nine years after the Bab's Declaration that Baha-'ullah gathered together the Babis at Baghdad, and began to teach them, and that at the end of the nineteenth year from the Declaration of the Bab, Baha-'ullah declared his Manifestation.

Another difficulty arises. The Bab does not always say the same thing. There are passages of the Persian Bayan which imply an interval between

---

[1] *Star of the West*, 1913, p. 238.

his own theophany and the next parallel to that which separated his own theophany from Muhammad's. He says, for instance, in *Wahid* II. Bab 17, according to Professor Browne,

'If he [whom God shall manifest] shall appear in the number of Ghiyath (1511) and all shall enter in, not one shall remain in the Fire. If He tarry [until the number of] Mustaghath (2001), all shall enter in, not one shall remain in the Fire.' [1]

I quote next from *Wahid* III. Bab 15:--

'None knoweth [the time of] the Manifestation save God: whenever it takes place, all must believe and must render thanks to God, although it is hoped of His Grace that He will come ere [the number of] Mustaghath, and will raise up the Word of God on his part. And the Proof is only a sign [or verse], and His very Existence proves Him, since all also is known by Him, while He cannot be known by what is below Him. Glorious is God above that which they ascribe to Him.' [2]

Elsewhere (vii. 9), we are told vaguely that the Advent of the Promised One will be sudden, like that of the Point or Bab (iv. 10); it is an element of the great Oriental myth of the winding-up of the old cycle and the opening of a new. [3]

A Bahai scholar furnishes me with another passage--

'God knoweth in what age He will manifest him. But from the springing (beginning) of the manifestation to its head (perfection) are nineteen years.' [4]

This implies a preparation period of nineteen years, and if we take this statement with a parallel one, we can, I think, have no doubt that the Bab expected the assumption, not immediate however, of the reins of

---

[1] *History of the Babis*, edited by E. G. Browne; Introd. p. xxvi. Traveller's Narrative (Browne), Introd. p. xvii.
[2] *History of the Babis*, Introd. p. xxx.
[3] Cheyne, *Mines of Isaiah Re-explored*, Index, 'Myth.'
[4] Bayan, *Wahid*, III., chap. iii.

government by the Promised One. The parallel statement is as follows, according to the same Bahai scholar.

'God only knoweth his age. But the time of his proclamation after mine is the number Wahid (=19, cabbalistically), and whenever he cometh during this period, accept him.' [1]

Another passage may be quoted by the kindness of Mirza 'Ali Akbar. It shows that the Bab has doubts whether the Great Manifestation will occur in the lifetime of Baha-'ullah and Subh-i-Ezel (one or other of whom is addressed by the Bab in this letter). The following words are an extract:--

'And if God hath not manifested His greatness in thy days, then act in accordance with that which hath descended (i.e. been revealed), and never change a word in the verses of God.

'This is the order of God in the Sublime Book; ordain in accordance with that which hath descended, and never change the orders of God, that men may not make variations in God's religion.'

NON-FINALITY OF REVELATION

Not less important than the question of the Bab's appointment of his successor is that of his own view of the finality or non-finality of his revelation. The Bayan does not leave this in uncertainty. The Kur'an of the Babis expressly states that a new Manifestation takes place whenever there is a call for it (ii. 9, vi. 13); successive revelations are like the same sun arising day after day (iv. 12, vii. 15, viii. 1). The Bab's believers therefore are not confined to a revelation constantly becoming less and less applicable to the spiritual wants of the present age. And very large discretionary powers are vested in 'Him whom He will make manifest,' extending even to the abrogation of the commands of the Bayan (iii. 3).

EARLY CHRISTIANITY AND BAHAISM AND BUDDHISM

The comparisons sometimes drawn between the history of nascent Christianity and that of early Bahaism are somewhat misleading. 'Ali Muhammad of Shiraz was more than a mere forerunner of the Promised

---

[1] Bayan, *Brit. Mus. Text*, p. 151.

Saviour; he was not merely John the Baptist--he was the Messiah, All-wise and Almighty, himself. True, he was of a humble mind, and recognized that what he might ordain would not necessarily be suitable for a less transitional age, but the same may be said--if our written records may be trusted--of Jesus Christ. For Jesus was partly his own forerunner, and antiquated his own words.

It is no doubt a singular coincidence that both 'Ali Muhammad and Jesus Christ are reported to have addressed these words to a disciple: 'To-day thou shalt be with me in Paradise.' But if the Crucifixion is unhistorical--and there is, I fear, considerable probability that it is--what is the value of this coincidence?

More important is it that both in early Christianity and in early Bahaism we find a conspicuous personage who succeeds in disengaging the faith from its particularistic envelope. In neither case is this personage a man of high culture or worldly position. [1] This, I say, is most important. Paul and Baha-'ullah may both be said to have transformed their respective religions. Yet there is a difference between them. Baha-'ullah and his son Abdul-Baha after him were personal centres of the new covenant; Paul was not.

This may perhaps suffice for the parallels--partly real, partly supposed--between early Christianity and early Bahaism. I will now refer to an important parallel between the development of Christianity and that of Buddhism. It is possible to deny that the Christianity of Augustine [2] deserves its name, on the ground of the wide interval which exists between his religious doctrines and the beliefs of Jesus Christ. Similarly, one may venture to deny that the Mahâyâna developments of Buddhism are genuine products of the religion because they contain some elements derived from other Indian systems. In both cases, however, grave injustice would be done by any such assumption. It is idle 'to question the historical value of an organism which is now full of vitality and active in all its functions, and to treat it like an archaeological object, dug out from the depths of the earth, or like a piece of bric-à-brac, discovered in the ruins of an ancient royal palace. Mahâyânaism is not an object of historical curiosity. Its vitality and activity concern us in our daily life. It is a great

---

[1] Leslie Johnston's phraseology (*Some Alternatives to Jesus Christ*, p. 114) appears to need revision.
[2] Professor Anesaki of Tokio regards Augustine as the Christian Nagarjuna.

spiritual organism. What does it matter, then, whether or not Mahâyânaism is the genuine teaching of the Buddha?' [1] The parallel between the developments of these two great religions is unmistakable. We Christians insist--and rightly so--on the 'genuineness' of our own religion in spite of the numerous elements unknown to its 'Founder.' The northern Buddhism is equally 'genuine,' being equally true to the spirit of the Buddha.

It is said that Christianity, as a historical religion, contrasts with the most advanced Buddhism. But really it is no loss to the Buddhist Fraternity if the historical element in the life of the Buddha has retired into the background. A cultured Buddhist of the northern section could not indeed admit that he has thrust the history of Gautama entirely aside, but he would affirm that his religion was more philosophical and practically valuable than that of his southern brothers, inasmuch as it transcended the boundary of history. In a theological treatise called *Chin-kuang-ming* we read as follows: 'It would be easier to count every drop of water in the ocean, or every grain of matter that composes a vast mountain than to reckon the duration of the life of Buddha.' 'That is to say, Buddha's life does not belong to the time-series: Buddha is the "I Am" who is above time.' [2] And is not the Christ of Christendom above the world of time and space? Lastly, must not both Christians and Buddhists admit that among the Christs or Buddhas the most godlike are those embodied in narratives as Jesus and Gautama?

WESTERN AND EASTERN RELIGION

Religion, as conceived by most Christians of the West, is very different from the religion of India. Three-quarters of it (as Matthew Arnold says) has to do with conduct; it is a code with a very positive and keen divine sanction. Few of its adherents, indeed, have any idea of the true position of morality, and that the code of Christian ethics expresses barely one half of the religious idea. The other half (or even more) is expressed in assurances of holy men that God dwells within us, or even that we are God. A true morality helps us to realize this--morality is not to be tied up and labelled, but is identical with the cosmic as well as individual principle of Love. Sin (i.e. an unloving disposition) is to be avoided because it blurs the outlines of the Divine Form reflected, however dimly, in each of us.

---

[1] Suzuki, *Outlines of Mahâyâna Buddhism*, p. 15.
[2] Johnston, *Buddhist China*, p. 114.

There are, no doubt, a heaven where virtue is rewarded, and a hell where vice is punished, for the unphilosophical minds of the vulgar. But the only reward worthy of a lover of God is to get nearer and nearer to Him. Till the indescribable goal (Nirvana) is reached, we must be content with realizing. This is much easier to a Hindu than to an Englishman, because the former has a constant sense of that unseen power which pervades and transcends the universe. I do not understand how Indian seekers after truth can hurry and strive about sublunary matters. Surely they ought to feel 'that this tangible world, with its chatter of right and wrong, subserves the intangible.'

Hard as it must be for the adherents of such different principles to understand each other, it is not, I venture to think, impossible. And, as at once an Anglican Christian and an adopted Brahmaist, I make the attempt to bring East and West religiously together.

RELIGIOUS TEACHERS OF THE EAST

The greatest religious teachers and reformers who have appeared in recent times are (if I am not much mistaken) Baha-'ullah the Persian and Keshab Chandra Sen the Indian. The one began by being a reformer of the Muhammadan society or church, the other by acting in the same capacity for the Indian community and more especially for the Brahmo Samaj--a very imperfect and loosely organized religious society or church founded by Rammohan Roy. By a natural evolution the objects of both reformers were enlarged; both became the founders of world-churches, though circumstances prevented the extension of the Brotherhood of the New Dispensation beyond the limits of India.

In both cases a doubt has arisen in the minds of some spectators whether the reformers have anything to offer which has not already been given by the Hebrew prophets and by the finest efflorescence of these--Jesus Christ. I am bound to express the opinion that they have. Just as the author of the Fourth Gospel looks forward to results of the Dispensation of the Spirit which will outdo those of the Ministry of Jesus (John xiv. 12), so we may confidently look forward to disclosures of truth and of depths upon depths of character which will far surpass anything that could, in the Nearer or Further East, have been imagined before the time of Baha-'ullah.

I do not say that Baha-'ullah is unique or that His revelations are final. There will be other Messiahs after Him, nor is the race of the prophets extinct. The supposition of finality is treason to the ever active, ever creative Spirit of Truth. But till we have already entered upon a new aeon, we shall have to look back in a special degree to the prophets who introduced our own aeon, Baha-'ullah and Keshab Chandra Sen, whose common object is the spiritual unification of all peoples. For it is plain that this union of peoples can only be obtained through the influence of prophetic personages, those of the past as well as those of the present.

QUALITIES OF THE MEN OF THE COMING RELIGION (Gal. v. 22)

1. Love. What is love? Let Rabindranath Tagore tell us.

'In love all the contradictions of existence merge themselves and are lost. Only in love are unity and duality not at variance. Love must be one and two at the same time.

'Only love is motion and rest in one. Our heart ever changes its place till it finds love, and then it has its rest....

'In this wonderful festival of creation, this great ceremony of self-sacrifice of God, the lover constantly gives himself up to gain himself in love....

'In love, at one of its poles you find the personal, and at the other the impersonal.' [1]

I do not think this has been excelled by any modern Christian teacher, though the vivid originality of the Buddha's and of St. Paul's descriptions of love cannot be denied. The subject, however, is too many-sided for me to attempt to describe it here. Suffice it to say that the men of the coming religion will be distinguished by an intelligent and yet intense altruistic affection--the new-born love.

2 and 3. Joy and Peace. These are fundamental qualities in religion, and especially, it is said, in those forms of religion which appear to centre in incarnations. This statement, however, is open to criticism. It matters but little how we attain to joy and peace, as long as we do attain to them.

---

[1] Tagore, *Sadhana* (1913), p. 114.

Christians have not surpassed the joy and peace produced by the best and safest methods of the Indian and Persian sages.

I would not belittle the tranquil and serene joy of the Christian saint, but I cannot see that this is superior to the same joy as it is exhibited in the Psalms of the Brethren or the Sisters in the Buddhistic Order. Nothing is more remarkable in these songs than the way in which joy and tranquillity are interfused. So it is with God, whose creation is the production of tranquillity and utter joy, and so it is with godlike men--men such as St. Francis of Assisi in the West and the poet-seers of the Upanishads in the East. All these are at once joyous and serene. As Tagore says, 'Joy without the play of joy is no joy; play without activity is no play.' [1] And how can he act to advantage who is perturbed in mind? In the coming religion all our actions will be joyous and tranquil. Meantime, transitionally, we have much need both of long-suffering [2] and of courage; 'quit you like men, be strong.' (I write in August 1914.)

REFORM OF ISLAM

And what as to Islam? Is any fusion between this and the other great religions possible? A fusion between Islam and Christianity can only be effected if first of all these two religions (mutually so repugnant) are reformed. Thinking Muslims will more and more come to see that the position assigned by Muhammad to himself and to the Kur'an implies that he had a thoroughly unhistorical mind. In other words he made those exclusive and uncompromising claims under a misconception. There were true apostles or prophets, both speakers and writers, between the generally accepted date of the ministry of Jesus and that of the appearance of Muhammad, and these true prophets were men of far greater intellectual grasp than the Arabian merchant.

Muslim readers ought therefore to feel it no sacrilege if I advocate the correction of what has thus been mistakenly said. Muhammad was one of the prophets, not *the* prophet (who is virtually = the Logos), and the Kur'an is only adapted for Arabian tribes, not for all nations of the world.

---

[1] Tagore, *Sadhana* (1913), p. 131.
[2] This quality is finely described in chap. vi. of *The Path of Light* (Wisdom of the East series).

One of the points in the exhibition of which the Arabian Bible is most imperfect is the love of God, i.e. the very point in which the Sufi classical poets are most admirable, though indeed an Arabian poetess, who died 135 Hij., expresses herself already in the most thrilling tones. [1]

Perhaps one might be content, so far as the Kur'an is concerned, with a selection of Suras, supplemented by extracts from other religious classics of Islam. I have often thought that we want both a Catholic Christian lectionary and a Catholic prayer-book. To compile this would be the work not of a prophet, but of a band of interpreters. An exacting work which would be its own reward, and would promote, more perhaps than anything else, the reformation and ultimate blending of the different religions.

Meantime no persecution should be allowed in the reformed Islamic lands. Thankful as we may be for the Christian and Bahaite heroism generated by a persecuting fanaticism, we may well wish that it might be called forth otherwise. Heroic was the imprisonment and death of Captain Conolly (in Bukhara), but heroic also are the lives of many who have spent long years in unhealthy climates, to civilize and moralize those who need their help.

SYNTHESIS OF RELIGIONS

'There is one God and Father of all, who is over all, and through all, and in all.'

These words in the first instance express the synthesis of Judaism and Oriental pantheism, but may be applied to the future synthesis of Islam and Hinduism, and of both conjointly with Christianity. And the subjects to which I shall briefly refer are the exclusiveness of the claims of Christ and of Muhammad, and of Christ's Church and of Muhammad's, the image-worship of the Hindus and the excessive development of mythology in Hinduism. With the lamented Sister Nivedita I hold that, in India, in proportion as the two faiths pass into higher phases, the easier it becomes for the one faith to be brought into a synthesis combined with the other.

Sufism, for instance, is, in the opinion of most, 'a Muhammadan sect.' It must, at any rate, be admitted to have passed through several stages, but there is, I think, little to add to fully developed Sufism to make it an ideal

---

[1] Von Kremer's *Herrschende Ideen des Islams*, pp. 64, etc.

synthesis of Islam and Hinduism. That little, however, is important. How can the Hindu accept the claim either of Christ or of Muhammad to be the sole gate to the mansions of knowledge?

The most popular of the Hindu Scriptures expressly provides for a succession of *avatârs*; how, indeed, could the Eternal Wisdom have limited Himself to raising up a single representative of Messiahship. For were not Sakya Muni, Kabir and his disciple Nanak, Chaitanya, the Tamil poets (to whom Dr. Pope has devoted himself) Messiahs for parts of India, and Nisiran for Japan, not to speak here of Islamic countries?

It is true, the exclusive claim of Christ (I assume that they are adequately proved) is not expressly incorporated into the Creeds, so that by mentally recasting the Christian can rid himself of his burden. And a time must surely come when, by the common consent of the Muslim world the reference to Muhammad in the brief creed of the Muslim will be removed. For such a removal would be no disparagement to the prophet, who had, of necessity, a thoroughly unhistorical mind (p. 113).

The 'one true Church' corresponds of course with the one true God. Hinduism, which would willingly accept the one, would as naturally accept the other also, as a great far-spreading caste. There are in fact already monotheistic castes in Hinduism.

As for image-worship, the Muslims should not plume themselves too much on their abhorrence of it, considering the immemorial cult of the Black Stone at Mecca. If a conference of Vedantists and Muslims could be held, it would appear that the former regarded image-worship (not idolatry) [1]simply as a provisional concession to the ignorant masses, who will not perhaps always remain so ignorant. So, then, Image-worship and its attendant Mythology have naturally become intertwined with high and holy associations. Thus that delicate poetess Mrs. Naidu (by birth a Parsi) writes:

> Who serves her household in fruitful pride,
> And worships the gods at her husband's side.

---

[1] Idols and images are not the same thing; the image is, or should be, symbolic. So, at least, I venture to define it.

I do not see, therefore, why we Christians (who have a good deal of myth in our religion) should object to a fusion with Islam and Hinduism on the grounds mentioned above. Only I do desire that both the Hindu and the Christian myths should be treated symbolically. On this (so far as the former are concerned) I agree with Keshab Chandra Sen in the last phase of his incomplete religious development. That the myths of Hinduism require sifting, cannot, I am sure, be denied.

From myths to image-worship is an easy step. What is the meaning of the latter? The late Sister Nivedita may help us to find an answer. She tells us that when travelling ascetics go through the villages, and pause to receive alms, they are in the habit of conversing on religious matters with the good woman of the house, and that thus even a bookless villager comes to understand the truth about images. We cannot think, however, that all will be equally receptive, calling to mind that even in our own country multitudes of people substitute an unrealized doctrine about Christ for Christ Himself (i.e. convert Christ into a church doctrine), while others invoke Christ, with or without the saints, in place of God.

Considering that Christendom is to a large extent composed of image-worshippers, why should there not be a synthesis between Hinduism and Islam on the one hand, and Hinduism, Buddhism, Islam, and Christianity on the other? The differences between these great religions are certainly not slight. But when we get behind the forms, may we not hope to find some grains of the truth? I venture, therefore, to maintain the position occupied above as that to which Indian religious reformers must ultimately come.

I do not deny that Mr. Farquhar has made a very good fight against this view. The process of the production of an image is, to us, a strange one. It is enough to mention the existence of a rite of the bringing of life into the idol which marks the end of that process. But there are many very educated Hindus who reject with scorn the view that the idol has really been made divine, and the passage quoted by Mr. Farquhar (p. 335) from Vivekananda [1] seems to me conclusive in favour of the symbol theory.

It would certainly be an aesthetic loss if these artistic symbols disappeared. But the most precious jewel would still remain, the Being who is in Himself

---

[1] Sister Nivedita's teacher.

unknowable, but who is manifested in the Divine Logos or Sofia and in a less degree in the prophets and Messiahs.

INCARNATIONS

There are some traces both in the Synoptics and in the Fourth Gospel of a Docetic view of the Lord's Person, in other words that His humanity was illusory, just as, in the Old Testament, the humanity of celestial beings is illusory. The Hindus, however, are much more sure of this. The reality of an incarnation would be unworthy of a God. And, strange as it may appear to us, this Docetic theory involves no pain or disappointment for the believer, who does but amuse himself with the sports [1] of his Patron. At the same time he is very careful not to take the God as a moral example; the result of this would be disastrous. The *avatâr* is super-moral. [2]

What, then, was the object of the *avatâr*? Not simply to amuse. It was, firstly, to win the heart of the worshipper, and secondly, to communicate that knowledge in which is eternal life.

And what is to be done, in the imminent sifting of Scriptures and Traditions, with these stories? They must be rewritten, just as, I venture to think, the original story of the God-man Jesus was rewritten by being blended with the fragments of a biography of a great and good early Jewish teacher. The work will be hard, but Sister Nivedita and Miss Anthon have begun it. It must be taken as a part of the larger undertaking of a selection of rewritten myths.

Is Baha-'ullah an *avatâr*? There has no doubt been a tendency to worship him. But this tendency need not be harmful to sanity of intellect. There are various degrees of divinity. Baha-'ullah's degree maybe compared to St. Paul's. Both these spiritual heroes were conscious of their superiority to ordinary believers; at the same time their highest wish was that their disciples might learn to be as they were themselves. Every one is the temple of the holy (divine) Spirit, and this Spirit-element must be deserving of worship. It is probable that the Western training of the objectors is the

---

[1] See quotation from the poet Tulsi Das in Farquhar, *The Crown of Hinduism*, p. 431.
[2] See Farquhar, p. 434.

cause of the opposition in India to some of the forms of honour lavished, in spite of his dissuasion, on Keshab Chandra Sen.[1]

IS JESUS UNIQUE?

One who has 'learned Christ' from his earliest years finds a difficulty in treating the subject at the head of this section. 'The disciple is not above his Master,' and when the Master is so far removed from the ordinary--is, in fact, the regenerator of society and of the individual,--such a discussion seems almost more than the human mind can undertake. And yet the subject has to be faced, and if Paul 'learned' a purely ideal Christ, deeply tinged with the colours of mythology, why should not we follow Paul's example, imitating a Christ who put on human form, and lived and died for men as their Saviour and Redeemer? Why should we not go even beyond Paul, and honour God by assuming a number of Christs, among whom--if we approach the subject impartially--would be Socrates, Zarathustra, Gautama the Buddha, as well as Jesus the Christ?

Why, indeed, should we not? If we consider that we honour God by assuming that every nation contains righteous men, accepted of God, why should we not complete our theory by assuming that every nation also possesses prophetic (in some cases more than prophetic) revealers? Some rather lax historical students may take a different view, and insist that we have a trustworthy tradition of the life of Jesus, and that 'if in that historical figure I cannot see God, then I am without God in the world.'[2] It is, however, abundantly established by criticism that most of what is contained even in the Synoptic Gospels is liable to the utmost doubt, and that what may reasonably be accepted is by no means capable of use as the basis of a doctrine of Incarnation. I do not, therefore, see why the Life of Jesus should be a barrier to the reconciliation of Christianity and Hinduism. Both religions in their incarnation theories are, as we shall see (taking Christianity in its primitive form), frankly Docetic, both assume a fervent love for the manifesting God on the part of the worshipper. I cannot, however, bring myself to believe that there was anything, even in the most primitive form of the life of the God-man Jesus, comparable to the *unmoral* story of the life of Krishna. Small wonder that many of the Vaishnavas prefer the *avatâr* of Rama.

---

[1] *Life and Teachings of Keshub Chunder Sen*, pp. III ff.
[2] Leslie Johnston, *Some Alternatives to Jesus Christ*, p. 199.

It will be seen, therefore, that it is impossible to discuss the historical character of the Life of Jesus without soon passing into the subject of His uniqueness. It is usual to suppose that Jesus, being a historical figure, must also be unique, and an Oxford theologian remarks that 'we see the Spirit in the Church always turning backwards to the historical revelation and drawing only thence the inspiration to reproduce it.'[1] He thinks that for the Christian consciousness there can be only one Christ, and finds this to be supported by a critical reading of the text of the Gospels. Only one Christ! But was not the Buddha so far above his contemporaries and successors that he came to be virtually deified? How is not this uniqueness? It is true, Christianity has, thus far, been intolerant of other religions, which contrasts with the 'easy tolerance' of Buddhism and Hinduism and, as the author may wish to add, of Bahaism. But is the Christian intolerance a worthy element of character? Is it consistent with the Beatitude pronounced (if it was pronounced) by Jesus on the meek? May we not, with Mr. L. Johnston's namesake, fitly say, 'Such notions as these are a survival from the bad old days'?[2]

THE SPIRIT OF GOD

Another very special jewel of Christianity is the doctrine of *the Spirit*. The term, which etymologically means 'wind,' and in Gen. i. 2 and Isa. xl. 13 appears to be a fragment of a certain divine name, anciently appropriated to the Creator and Preserver of the world, was later employed for the God who is immanent in believers, and who is continually bringing them into conformity with the divine model. With the Brahmaist theologian, P.C. Mozoomdar, I venture to think that none of the old divine names is adequately suggestive of the functions of the Spirit. The Spirit's work is, in fact, nothing short of re-creation; His creative functions are called into exercise on the appearance of a new cosmic cycle, which includes the regeneration of souls.

I greatly fear that not enough homage has been rendered to the Spirit in this important aspect. And yet the doctrine is uniquely precious because of the great results which have already, in the ethical and intellectual spheres, proceeded from it, and of the still greater ones which faith descries in the future. We have, I fear, not yet done justice to the spiritual capacities with

---

[1] Leslie Johnston, *op. cit.* pp. 200 f.
[2] Johnston, *Buddhist China*, p. 306.

which we are endowed. I will therefore take leave to add, following Mozoomdar, that no name is so fit for the indwelling God as Living Presence.¹ His gift to man is life, and He Himself is Fullness of Life. The idea therefore of God, in the myth of the Dying and Reviving Saviour, is, from one point of view, imperfect. At any rate it is a more constant help to think of God as full, not of any more meagre satisfaction at His works, but of the most intense joy.

Let us, then, join our Indian brethren in worshipping God the Spirit. In honouring the Spirit we honour Jesus, the mythical and yet real incarnate God. The Muhammadans call Jesus *ruhu'llah*, 'the Spirit of God,' and the early Bahais followed them. One of the latter addressed these striking words to a traveller from Cambridge: 'You (i.e. the Christian Church) are to-day the Manifestation of Jesus; you are the Incarnation of the Holy Spirit; nay, did you but realize it, you are God.' ² I fear that this may go too far for some, but it is only a step in advance of our Master, St. Paul. If we do not yet fully realize our blessedness, let us make it our chief aim to do so. How God's Spirit can be dwelling in us and we in Him, is a mystery, but we may hope to get nearer and nearer to its meaning, and see that it is no *Maya*, no illusion. As an illustration of the mystery I will quote this from one of Vivekananda's lectures. ³

'Young men of Lahore, raise once more that wonderful banner of Advaita, for on no other ground can you have that all-embracing love, until you see that the same Lord is present in the same manner everywhere; unfurl that banner of love. "Arise, awake, and stop not till the goal is reached." Arise, arise once more, for nothing can be done without renunciation. If you want to help others, your own little self must go.... At the present time there are men who give up the world to help their own salvation. Throw away everything, even your own salvation, and go and help others.'

CHINESE AND JAPANESE RELIGION

It is much to be wished that Western influence on China may not be exerted in the wrong way, i.e. by an indiscriminate destruction of religious tradition. Hitherto the three religions of China--Confucianism, Taoism, and

---

¹ Mozoomdar, *The Spirit of God* (1898), p. 64.
² E.G. Browne, *A Year among the Persians*, p. 492.
³ *Jnana Yoga*, p. 154.

Buddhism--have been regarded as forming one organism, and as equally necessary to the national culture. Now, however, there is a danger that this hereditary union may cease, and that, in their disunited state, the three cults may be destined in course of time to disappear and perish. Shall they give place to dogmatic Christianity or, among the most cultured class, to agnosticism? Would it not be better to work for the retention at any rate of Buddhism and Confucianism in a purified form? My own wish would be that the religious-ethical principles of Buddhism should be applied to the details of civic righteousness. The work could only be done by a school, but by the co-operation of young and old it could be done.

Taoism, however, is doomed, unless some scientifically trained scholar (perhaps a Buddhist) will take the trouble to sift the grain from the chaff. As Mr. Johnston tells us, [1] the opening of every new school synchronizes with the closing of a Taoist temple, and the priests of the cult are not only despised by others, but are coming to despise themselves. Lao-Tze, however, has still his students, and accretions can hardly be altogether avoided. Chinese Buddhism, too, has accretions, both philosophic and religious, and unless cleared of these, we cannot hope that Buddhism will take its right place in the China of the future. Suzuki, however, in his admirable *Outlines of Mahayana Buddhism*, has recognized and expounded (as I at least think) the truest Buddhism, and it is upon him I chiefly rely in my statements in the present work.

There is no accretion, however, in the next point which I shall mention. The noble altruism of the Buddhism of China and Japan must at no price be rejected from the future religion of those countries, but rather be adopted as a model by us Western Christians. Now there are three respects in which (among others) the Chinese and Japanese may set us an example. Firstly, their freedom from self, and even from pre-occupying thoughts of personal salvation. Secondly, the perception that in the Divine Manifestation there must be a feminine element (*das ewig-weibliche*). And thirdly, the possibility of vicarious moral action. On the first, I need only remark that one of those legends of Sakya Muni, which are so full of moral meaning, is beautified by this selflessness. On the second, that Kuan-yin or Kwannon, though formerly a god, [2] the son of the Buddha Amitâbha, is now regarded

---

[1] *Buddhist China*, p. 12.
[2] 'God' and 'Goddess' are of course unsuitable. Read *pusa*.

as a goddess, 'the All-compassionate, Uncreated Saviour, the Royal Bodhisat, who (like the Madonna) hears the cries of the world.'[1]

But it is the third point which chiefly concerns us here because of the great spiritual comfort which it conveys. It is the possibility of doing good in the name of some beloved friend or relative and to 'turn over' (*parimarta*) one's *karma* to this friend. The extent to which this idea is pressed may, to some, be bewildering. Even the bliss of Nirvana is to be rejected that the moral and physical sufferings of the multitude may be relieved. This is one of the many ways in which the Living Presence is manifested.

GOD-MAN

Tablet of Ishrakat (p. 5).--Praise be to God who manifested the Point and sent forth from it the knowledge of what was and is (i.e. all things); who made it (the Point) the Herald in His Name, the Precursor to His Most Great Manifestation, by which the nerves of nations have quivered with fear and the Light has risen from the horizon of the world. Verily it is that Point which God hath made to be a Sea of Light for the sincere among His servants, and a ball of fire for the deniers among His creations and the impious among His people.--This shows that Baha-'ullah did not regard the so-called Bab as a mere forerunner.

The want of a surely attested life, or extract from a life, of a God-man will be more and more acutely felt. There is only one such life; it is that of Baha-'ullah. Through Him, therefore, let us pray in this twentieth century amidst the manifold difficulties which beset our social and political reconstructions; let Him be the prince-angel who conveys our petitions to the Most High. The standpoint of Immanence, however, suggests a higher and a deeper view. Does a friend need to ask a favour of a friend? Are we not in Baha'ullah ('the Glory of God'), and is not He in God? Therefore, 'ye shall ask what ye will, and it shall be done unto you' (John xv. 7). Far be it that we should even seem to disparage the Lord Jesus, but the horizon of His early worshippers is too narrow for us to follow them, and the critical difficulties are insuperable. The mirage of the ideal Christ is all that remains, when these obstacles have been allowed for.

---

[1] Johnston, *Buddhist China*, pp. 101, 273.

We read much about God-men in the narratives of the Old Testament, where the name attached to a manifestation of God in human semblance is 'malak Yahwè (Jehovah)' or 'malak Elohim'--a name of uncertain meaning which I have endeavoured to explain more correctly elsewhere. In the New Testament too there is a large Docetic element. Apparently a supernatural Being walks about on earth--His name is Jesus of Nazareth, or simply Jesus, or with a deifying prefix 'Lord' and a regal appendix 'Christ.' He has doubtless a heavenly message to individuals, but He has also one to the great social body. Christ, says Mr. Holley, is a perfect revelation for the individual, but not for the social organism. This is correct if we lay stress on the qualifying word 'perfect,' especially if we hold that St. Paul has the credit of having expanded and enriched the somewhat meagre representation of Christ in the Synoptic Gospels. It must be conceded that Baha-'ullah had a greater opportunity than Christ of lifting both His own and other peoples to a higher plane, but the ideal of both was the same.

Baha-'ullah and Christ, therefore, were both 'images of God';[1] God is the God of the human people as well as of individual men, so too is the God of whom Baha-'ullah is the reflection or image. Only, we must admit that Baha-'ullah had the advantage of centuries more of evolution, and that he had also perhaps more complex problems to solve.

And what as to 'Ali Muhammad of Shiraz? From a heavenly point of view, did he play a great *rôle* in the Persian Reformation? Let us listen to Baha-'ullah in the passage quoted above from the Tablet of Ishrakat.

PRAYER TO THE PERPETUAL CREATOR

O giver of thyself! at the vision of thee as joy let our souls flame up to thee as the fire, flow on to thee as the river, permeate thy being as the fragrance of the flower. Give us strength to love, to love fully, our life in its joys and sorrows, in its gains and losses, in its rise and fall. Let us have strength enough fully to see and hear thy universe, and to work with full vigour therein. Let us fully live the life thou hast given us, let us bravely take and bravely give. This is our prayer to thee. Let us once for all dislodge from our minds the feeble fancy that would make out thy joy to be a thing apart from action, thin, formless and unsustained. Wherever the peasant

---

[1] Bousset, *Kyrios-Christos*, p. 144. Christ is the 'image of God' (2 Cor. iv. 4; Col. i. 15); or simply 'the image' (Rom. viii. 29).

tills the hard earth, there does thy joy gush out in the green of the corn; wherever man displaces the entangled forest, smooths the stony ground, and clears for himself a homestead, there does thy joy enfold it in orderliness and peace.

O worker of the universe! We would pray to thee to let the irresistible current of thy universal energy come like the impetuous south wind of spring, let it come rushing over the vast field of the life of man, let it bring the scent of many flowers, the murmurings of many woodlands, let it make sweet and vocal the lifelessness of our dried-up soul-life. Let our newly awakened powers cry out for unlimited fulfilment in leaf and flower and fruit!--Tagore, Sadhana (p. 133).

THE OPPORTUNENESS OF BAHAISM

The opportuneness of the Baha movement is brought into a bright light by the following extract from a letter to the Master from the great Orientalist and traveller, Arminius Vambéry. Though born a Jew, he tells us that believers in Judaism were no better than any other professedly religious persons, and that the only hope for the future lay in the success of the efforts of Abdul Baha, whose supreme greatness as a prophet he fully recognizes. He was born in Hungary in March 1832, and met Abdul Baha at Buda-Pest in April 1913. The letter was written shortly after the interview; some may perhaps smile at its glowing Oriental phraseology, but there are some Oriental writers who really mean what they seem to mean, and one of these (an Oriental by adoption) is Vambéry.

'... The time of the meeting with your excellency, and the memory of the benediction of your presence, recurred to the memory of this servant, and I am longing for the time when I shall meet you again. Although I have travelled through many countries and cities of Islam, yet have I never met so lofty a character and so exalted a personage as Your Excellency, and I can bear witness that it is not possible to find such another. On this account I am hoping that the ideals and accomplishments of Your Excellency may be crowned with success and yield results under all conditions, because behind these ideals and deeds I easily discern the eternal welfare and prosperity of the world of humanity.

'This servant, in order to gain first-hand information and experience, entered into the ranks of various religions; that is, outwardly I became a

Jew, Christian, Mohammedan, and Zoroastrian. I discovered that the devotees of these various religions do nothing else but hate and anathematize each other, that all these religions have become the instruments of tyranny and oppression in the hands of rulers and governors, and that they are the causes of the destruction of the world of humanity.

'Considering these evil results, every person is forced by necessity to enlist himself on the side of Your Excellency and accept with joy the prospect of a fundamental basis for a universal religion of God being laid through your efforts.

'I have seen the father of Your Excellency from afar. I have realized the self-sacrifice and noble courage of his son, and I am lost in admiration.

'For the principles and aims of Your Excellency I express the utmost respect and devotion, and if God, the Most High, confers long life, I will be able to serve you under all conditions. I pray and supplicate this from the depths of my heart.--Your servant, VAMBERY.'

(Published in the *Egyptian Gazette*, Sept. 24, 1913, by Mrs. J. Stannard.)

BAHAI BIBLIOGRAPHY

BROWNE, Prof. E. G.--A *Traveller's Narrative*. Written to illustrate the Episode of the Bab. Cambridge, 1901.

The New History. Cambridge, 1893.

History of the Bábís. Compiled by Hájji Mírzá Jání of Káshán between the years A.D. 1850 and 1852. Leyden, 1910.

'Babism,' article in *Encyclopaedia of Religions*. Two Papers on Babism in *JRAS*. 1889.

CHASE, THORNTON.--*In Galilee*. Chicago, 1908.

DREYFUS, HIPPOLYTE.--*The Universal Religion; Bahaism*. 1909.

GOBINEAU, M. LE COMTE DE.--*Religions et Philosophies dans l'Asie Centrale*. Paris. 2nd edition, Paris, 1866.

HAMMOND, ERIC.--*The Splendour of God*. 1909.

HOLLEY, HORACE.--*The Modern Social Religion*. 1913.

HUART, CLEMENT.--*La Religion du Bab*. Paris, 1889.

NICOLAS, A. L. M.--*Seyy'ed Ali Mohammed, dit Le Bab*. Paris, 1905.

Le Béyân Arabe. Paris, 1905.

PHELPS, MYRON H.--*Life and Teachings of Abbas Effendi*. New York, 1914.

RÖMER, HERMANN.--*Die Babi-Beha'i, Die jüngste muhammedanische Sekte*. Potsdam, 1912.

RICE, W. A.--'Bahaism from the Christian Standpoint,' *East and West*, January 1913.

SKRINE, F. H.--*Bahaism, the Religion of Brotherhood and its place in the Evolution of Creeds*. 1912.

WILSON, S. G.--'The Claims of Bahaism,' *East and West*, July 1914.

Works of the BAB, BAHA-'ULLAH, ABDUL BAHA, and ABU'L FAZL:

L'Épître au Fils du Loup. Baha-'ullah. Traduction française par H. Dreyfus. Paris, 1913.

Le Beyan arabe. Nicolas. Paris, 1905.

The Hidden Words. Chicago, 1905.

The Seven Valleys. Chicago.

Livre de la Certitude. Dreyfus. Paris, 1904.

The Book of Ighan. Chicago.

Works of ABDUL BAHA:

Some Answered Questions. 1908.

Tablets. Vol. i. Chicago, 1912.

Work by MIRZA ABU'L FAZL:

The Brilliant Proof. Chicago, 1913.

LAUS DEO

Printed in the USA
CPSIA information can be obtained
at www.ICGtesting.com
CBHW051332291124
18172CB00041B/1003

9 781397 665362